Jeffrey Dahmer

The Milwaukee Cannibal

Savannah Crawford

Table of Contents

Prologue

With a tale of horror spanning thirteen years, few serial killers have matched Jeffrey Dahmer in morbid curiosity and in gore.

From 1978 to 1991, a real-life monster roamed the streets, becoming the stuff of nightmares. This phantom figure would later be dubbed *'The Milwaukee Monster'* and *'The Milwaukee Cannibal'*. The sheer gruesomeness of his crimes and the length of time he managed to evade the law made this serial killer's story both terrifying and fascinating.

Rape, murder, dismemberment, necrophilia, and cannibalism—Jeffrey Dahmer's crimes form a cornucopia of grisly madness, a collection of the vilest of atrocities a human being can commit against another.

For decades, psychological experts and crime specialists alike have delved into the study of serial killers, trying to find a unifying logic behind the unthinkable. The science is in its infancy, however, and while there have been developments significant enough to distinguish the sociopath from the psychopath, humanity has a long way to go in finding definitive answers.

For now, this book explores the same fundamental question, *why*, and paints the picture of both normalcy and enigma. A monster walked among us. How could he have escaped detection for so long?

Chapter One:

Early Life

O n May 21, 1960 in Milwaukee, Wisconsin, the firstborn son of Lionel Herbert and Joyce Dahmer was born into the world. Similarly to many serial killers, Jeffrey Lionel Dahmer was born to a family that, by all indications, seemed normal.

A chemistry student at Marquette University at the time, Lionel was finishing his degree and spending the rest of his time doting on his curious, exuberant child. In several interviews following the incarceration of his son, Lionel described Jeffrey as an outgoing little boy who loved to wrestle and play with the other kids. Grainy home videos showed a happy, mischievous child who made silly faces at the camera, unable to keep still for more than a few seconds. Little hands dug into the ground, caught dragonflies, or clutched onto the chains of a well-used swing.

Lionel recounted how his son was particularly tactile; Jeffrey fancied to touch and feel things, memorize how they felt against his skin, and explore the world through the roughness or smoothness of the little items he could hold. "He seemed to be very much in tune with what's around him. He just wanted to know what was going on," Lionel stated in one of the documentaries about his son.

This fascination translated to an interest in animals, which is made apparent in what is by all accounts an innocent anecdote that took on a grim tone in retrospect. Lionel was collecting the bones of dead animals from under the house, throwing them into a bucket. Jeffrey seemed to have been mesmerized by the soft, sharp clatter the bones made. He grabbed a handful and threw them into the bucket to hear the sound again.

Upon acquiring his PhD in chemistry, Lionel uprooted his family and they relocated to Ohio. After changing households three times, they settled on a two-acre property in the woods an hour's drive south of Cleveland. It was here that young Jeffrey seemed to become more withdrawn, retreating into his thoughts as he explored the new surroundings; rich with even more objects that nurtured his natural curiosity. To mitigate the stress of moving, his parents gifted Jeff with Frisky, a pet dog that would be the little boy's companion.

Soon after, another child was born into the family. In an effort to make their older son feel more involved, Lionel and Joyce allowed Jeff to name his little brother David.

The parents encouraged, almost coerced, the increasingly shy Jeff to socialize with other kids, but all he desired was to spend time with his father attending to their garden and raising livestock. A sweet letter written in the child's hand writing reads, "The squash and the pumpkins can never compare to the kind of dad who has curly hair. This poem is from Jeff, and I love you to death." The words are accompanied by a silly drawing of Lionel eating an ear of corn.

In the backdrop of this charmed childhood though was a slightly darker story. The Dahmer matriarch, who was a teletype machine instructor by profession, was known to have some mental conditions. Friends and neighbors described her as a tense woman whose neurosis presented as argumentative and attention-seeking behaviors. She liked to draw pity and surged herself into altercations over even the most trivial matters, especially with her husband. These fights sometimes turned violent, and the passive Lionel was ill-equipped to handle the situation. While Joyce was overemotional and fragile, her husband was cold, distant, and pusillanimous.

When Jeffrey entered the first grade, Joyce began to spend more time in bed, recovering from what can only be described as a general, inexplicable lethargy. Addicted to Equanil, she attempted suicide by overdose, putting even more stress on the household. Her husband was still working on his degree at the time, paired with a troubled wife, there was often little attention left for the young Jeffrey.

In Lionel Dahmer's 1994 book, '*A Father's Story*', he wrote a candid admission of his own avoidance of the toxic environment. He buried himself in work, often spending hours in the laboratory instead of tending to his family. And if that laboratory was the father's refuge, the son found his in the controlled realms of imagination. The boy often found himself in the woods, retreating into his thoughts in order to escape the fighting in the house.

Perhaps, all this time spent alone was what fostered intense introspective tendencies in a boy who was initially outgoing by nature. A child's imagination runs wild, and somewhere along the way, Jeffrey's seemed to have taken a dark turn. What evils lurked in the recesses of his mind, the world can only surmise, but what did manage to seep outside was nothing short of horrifying.

Chapter Two:

The Monster is Slow to Build

As the boy grew, so did his curiosity. His fascination with animals became a sinister portent for his future crimes. By his teenage years, it was no longer enough to observe these animals or feel the different textures of their outside bodies; he began to wonder how it all functioned within. He drove around looking for specimens, stuffing roadkill into garbage bags, and dissecting the carcasses in the woods behind his house.

At the same time that these macabre obsessions were taking root, puberty did its work. Physical changes were occurring, and desire and sexuality were developing. Jeff eventually realized that he was attracted to boys and men.

At the age of about fifteen or sixteen, he began to have obsessive fantasies of sex inclusive of violence. He thought about lying beside an unconscious man, feeling the weight of another body depressing the mattress, and wielding absolute power over this human being.

It wasn't long before this obsession consumed him enough to materialize into an actual scheme. A teenage Jeffrey plotted to use a baseball bat to bludgeon a local jogger whose trail he was familiar with. Fortunately, this jogger would never know how close to peril he was. He didn't show up on the expected day, and Jeffrey would never muster the nerve to try again.

Frustrated and unable to express and deal with the dark thoughts that plagued him, Jeffrey Dahmer retreated even further into himself and self-medicated with alcohol. Marty Schmidt, a former classmate, remembers asking him about the Styrofoam cup of scotch he had brought to an 8 AM class. He responded with a dismissive shaking of his shoulders. "It's my medicine," he'd said.

He never developed any close friendships and remained distant to his peers. To avoid getting picked on, he positioned himself as the class clown, pulling antics that were often so outrageous that "pulling a Dahmer" became a school colloquialism.

These displays of audacity weren't always disruptive, however. On a school trip to Washington, D.C. in his junior year, Jeff orchestrated a meeting with Vice President Walter Mondale by simply making a bold phone call. He explained that they were high school students from Ohio, in town for the week. By the end of that week, the class would have something very interesting to publish on the school newspaper.

Jeff did fairly well in school. Mike Kukral, another former classmate, described him as polite, respectful of authority, dressed nicely, and smart enough to achieve high marks when he wanted to— and did not seem to be all that different from other boys his age, and nobody could have recognized the monster lurking just beneath that façade of normalcy. The teenage hormones continued to rage parallel to repressed homosexual urges and a taste for violence.

It was like the perfect storm, so to speak. The deluge of sexual maturation combined with his morbid fantasies would later provide the theme for Jeffrey Dahmer's gruesome murders. In direct conflict with conventional—and now debunked—theories of what forms the minds of the world's most terrible criminals, it was neither abuse nor an early introduction to violence that created the nefarious Jeffrey Dahmer who hunted, killed, and raped his unsuspecting victims. It was in fact introspection that somehow built a bridge between death and sexual gratification.

Chapter Three:

A Bloody Christening

In 1978, only a few weeks after high school graduation, Jeffrey Dahmer would perform his own baptism of blood.

A series of life-altering changes paved the way for Dahmer's introduction into a life of turning dark fantasy into an even darker reality. His parents' troubled, tempestuous marriage dissolved into divorce, and his father moved out of the Ohio family home and into a motel. Without telling her ex-husband, Joyce took their younger son David and moved back to Wisconsin. Abandoned and directionless, the eighteen-year-old Jeffrey found himself alone, this time for a prolonged period.

The house seemed larger without the other occupants there. The silence was almost eerie, and the gentle rustling of the tree branches, a sound Jeffrey had grown up with, all of a sudden seemed strange and unfamiliar.

His mind wreaked havoc on his already fragile psyche, the deviant fantasies of sex and murder intensifying by the day, coming closer to breaking through the barriers of Jeff's inhibitions. Hormones and circumstance exacerbated the obsessions, and soon, a killer would be born. Dahmer would murder his first victim, an eighteen-year-old hitchhiker by the name of Steven Hicks.

Jeffrey picked him up from the side of the road and brought him to the newly emptied Dahmer home. In a later interview post-incarceration, Jeffrey recounted how he had initially driven past the young man but soon turned around to pick him up. He expresses regret in making this decision, as it kickstarted his life of crime. He attributes this moment to "when the nightmare became a reality."

Being of the same age, Jeffrey did not seem like a threat to the unassuming Steven Hicks. The promise of beer, companionship, and a comfortable place to rest for a while made it a rational decision to hop into the car of a stranger.

They pulled up to a house that was too big and empty for a lone eighteen-year-old to be living in. Nestled in the woods, it seemed a welcome respite from the noise of big cities and bustling towns. Big windows lined the walls of the house, and a raised deck faced the constantly humming forest that was the Dahmers' backyard.

They spent a few hours just "hanging out" and drinking beers until Hicks decided he was ready to leave. The threat of new abandonment and the resulting loneliness settled on Jeffrey's shoulders, heavy as lead. He knew he wouldn't be able to stand the thick silence of the empty house again, not when he'd just had a taste of what it felt like to have a friend again.

Jeffrey took a barbell, tested the weight of it in his hand, and let the fantasies he had lived with for years take over. He bludgeoned Steven, knocking him out in one blow, and wrapped his hands around the other boy's neck. He began to squeeze, feeling the flesh contract under his fingers, watching Steven's body fight for air even as it remained unconscious. It seemed like forever, but it would soon be over.

What occurred directly afterwards, the world can only guess, but what is known is that Dahmer had enough of a grasp on his senses to realize that he had committed a murder -- a crime. Hiding the evidence was the next logical step to the mad reality.

It was the middle of the night, and the deepening darkness emboldened him. Employing his experience in dissecting animals, he dismembered Hicks' body with a carving knife and threw them into garbage bags, performing the grisly task with terrifying precision. He loaded the bags into his car and headed for the dumpsite.

Distracted and still reeling from the alcohol, he was stopped by a police officer for drifting across the center line. The officer asked him what he was doing out so late and what the bags contained. Calm and collected, Dahmer replied with the lie his efficient mind had already concocted. He said he was dealing with his parents' divorce and had trouble sleeping; a quick drive and a trip to the dump would distract him for a while and be a welcome reprieve from the situation. It was a simple lie laced with a smidgen of truth, which is the most convincing kind. Amazingly, the officer bought it and sent him off with nothing but a ticket.

Rattled by the encounter, Jeff drove back home and thought of what to do. He separated flesh from bone and buried them in a crawlspace beneath the house. Two weeks later, the newly christened murderer would retrieve the bones and attempt to pulverize them. He took a sledgehammer and managed to crush them into small pieces. He scattered these fragments all over the woods that were his backyard, disguising them among the twigs, the fallen leaves, and the earth..

Chapter Four:

The 9-Year Aftermath

Oblivious to his son's recent tribulations, Lionel did not visit the family home until August. He was surprised to find his ex-wife and younger son absent. Concerned that his eldest was living alone and more than familiar with Jeff's tendency to become withdrawn and anti-social, the Dahmer patriarch moved back in and encouraged his son to find a job. No amount of encouragement, however, would be enough to get the young man interested. Day in and day out, Jeffrey sulked in the house, drowning himself in alcohol, destructive thoughts, and his secret guilt.

Desperate to help his son, Lionel took him to AA (Alcoholics Anonymous) meetings and counseling sessions, all of which proved futile. Jeffrey was too far gone, his gnawing secret weighing more heavily on his spirit than either his father or the therapists could imagine.

In an effort to pull his son out of the quicksand of alcoholism, Lionel enrolled Jeff in Ohio State University, hoping that college would give the boy a purpose, some semblance of direction. In return, Jeff spent the first semester drinking himself into further oblivion. So deep was he in his addiction that he became a regular at plasma centers, selling his blood, and buying beer with the money he earned.

It wasn't long before Jeffrey was kicked out of the university. More lost than ever before, he moved back home to face his frustrated, disappointed, and helpless father. "The doors are closing," Lionel said.

As a last, desperate attempt to get his son back on track, Lionel urged him to enlist in the Armed Forces. Perhaps being in the military would instill some discipline in the young man and force his drinking habits out of him. Uncaring and unopinionated about his own life, Jeffrey simply did as he was told and enlisted.

After completing his training, Jeff was assigned as a field medic, a role that expanded even more on his knowledge of the human anatomy. Unsurprisingly, he took to the position like a fish took to water, and he found himself enthusiastic about something for the first time in what seemed like forever. He responded well to authority, routine, and discipline, and a mere six months in the army brought forth the exuberant, outgoing Jeff of his childhood.

The positive outcome was short-lived, however, and when Jeff was sent to a tour of duty in Germany, his old habits resurfaced. He was soon discharged for excessive drinking, a fact he could not hide from his peers and superiors.

Unwilling to come home and bring even more disappointment to his family, he instead headed straight for Miami Beach, Florida without sending word of his arrival and whereabouts. At first, he lived in a motel, finding work in a sandwich shop, but when his living costs exceeded his earnings, he was forced into homelessness. He slept on the beach, alone again except for the rats that often crawled over him. He woke up in terror countless times, brushing the audacious rodents off his body. He was drowning in a restless solitude again, this time with the waves hitting the shore as the soundtrack to his misery.

It didn't take him long to call home and ask to be rescued. Knowledgeable of his son's weaknesses and self-destructive patterns, Lionel refused to send him money and instead sent him a plane ticket back to Ohio. To the aging man's chagrin, it was a drunken Jeff that met him at the airport.

They were back to square one, and for a year, Lionel allowed Jeff to live with him, making every effort to help his son. Having run out of options and ideas, the desperate father sent Jeff to live with his grandparents in Milwaukee. There, the boy seemed to find a desire to get better and make something of his life. He went to church with his grandmother and found solace in religion, vilifying his own homosexual urges in accordance with his newfound faith. Repressing these "immoral" tendencies, however, intensified his murderous and violent fantasies.

He found a job at a blood bank, perhaps finding some macabre comfort in being surrounded by the substance. Later, he worked a night shift as a mixer at a chocolate factory.

For three years, Jeff settled into what he called "right-living." He donned the persona of a church-going, hardworking citizen, and did his best to leave behind his troubled past and illicit fantasies. As fate would have it, however, an innocuous trip to the library would be his undoing. Among the fragrant, aging books and the brown, wooden shelves, he was offered the "forbidden fruit" in the form of a note offering sexual favors. A man had discretely given it to him, and while Jeff mustered enough willpower to decline, he would later recognize the moment as that which reawakened his desires—sexual, violent, and murderous.

His thoughts zoned in on a fantasy that quickly grew in specificity. He wanted to lie with another man, someone completely submissive to him, there simply to fulfill his sexual desires. And for the first time, he acknowledged his own selfishness—that he didn't want to return the favor or bother with caring about the other person's needs.

Having had a taste of murder and its aftermaths before, he didn't immediately choose the same path. Instead, he stole a male store mannequin and hid it in his closet. At night, he would take it out to masturbate to, and to lie beside it, letting his fantasies run wild. He imagined its plastic chest heaving up and down, its empty eyes quivering with life. He ran his hands down its smooth, cold arms, his fingers gingerly tracing the manufactured muscle lines on its torso.

His grandmother eventually found the mannequin, however, and outraged by its implications, she made Jeff get rid of it. This did little to stamp out the young man's homosexual desires. He began to frequent porn shops and bath houses that specifically catered to men cruising for casual, easy sex.

After finding a willing partner, Jeff would slip drugs and sleeping pills into their drinks and waited for them to fall unconscious. Feeling completely in control over these men, he would lie beside them and watch their eyes flutter in their sleep. He didn't have to imagine their chests rising and falling this time, nor make up the way their limbs sometimes twitched in slumber. He listened to them breathe; he would put his ear against their chests to find the gentle thumping of their hearts, and move down to their stomachs to hear the substances churning inside.

This satisfied him for a short while, until the routine was put to an end by a man overdosing and ending up in the hospital for a week. Upon learning of the incident, the club blacklisted Jeff, forcing him to explore other avenues to express his sexuality and sate his appetites for the taboo.

The gay bars and discos of Milwaukee proved to be rife with illicit activities and participants emboldened by the cloak of darkness. Introverted and shy, nobody could have guessed that Jeffrey Dahmer had such an active nightlife, prowling Milwaukee's gay scene.

Good looks and a boyish charm made him something of a "catch" in the bars and nightclubs, and he found little trouble finding a man who would be interested in him. However, he had a type—tall, lean, handsome boys and men of varying ethnicities.

Chapter Five:

The Lost Victim

On November 20, 1987, nine years after his first murder, Jeffrey Dahmer was on one of his regular nightly prowls. He was having drinks at 219, a downtown club, whose neon pink signage burned bright in the cool night air. His eyes scanned the room for a potential target. It wasn't long before he was chatting up the 25-year-old Steven Tuomi. Thick-haired, handsome, and with a slightly lopsided smile, Tuomi was attractive to the selective Dahmer. Their initial chat became mild flirtation that intensified as the night wore on. Soon, Jeffrey would be convincing his new friend to spend the night with him.

Oblivious to the imminent danger, Tuomi agreed to head for the Ambassador Hotel, where Jeff had already rented a room for the night.

In candid confessions years later, Dahmer would claim to not have any intention of killing anyone that night. By the killer's own account, the two were having a particularly good time before Dahmer, in what is now known as his modus operandi, drugged the young man's drink and proceeded to rape him when he fell unconscious. When

Jeffrey was done, he simply lay beside his new victim and fell into what he described to authorities and investigators as a peaceful sleep.

The morning would prove much more turbulent, however, as Jeffrey woke up to find his arms bruised and Steven's cold, lifeless body beside him. Even in his confessions, Jeffrey claimed to have no recollection of the murder. All he knew was that there were bruises all over the corpse's chest—bruises so severe that the chest was black and blue—and blood dribbling from the corner of Steven's mouth.

Years later, Jeffrey would phrase his explanations as speculations to authorities. He must have been drunk out of his mind, he would tell them, and attempted to rip out Tuomi's heart right out of his chest. Weakened by the inebriation and without the use of knives, of course, Dahmer would not even succeed in breaking the other man's skin. Nevertheless, the beating proved fatal.

Frantic and desperate to cover up the crime, Jeffrey went out and bought a large suitcase, an inconspicuous object to carry in a hotel. He stuffed the body inside and simply carried it out. Disposing of it would prove to be slightly more difficult, but the most immediate course of action was to transport the body to his grandmother's house. For a week, he kept it there, trying to decide what to do. This wasn't his first rodeo, however, and because he was able to get away with his first murder all those years ago, he figured the same methods of disposal would prove just as effective.

First, he removed the head, arms, and legs, dividing the cadaver into more manageable pieces. Setting aside the head, which he intended to use for sexual gratification later on, he filleted the rest of the body, expertly separating flesh from bone. He threw the pieces of flesh in garbage bags and simply tossed them in with the rest of the trash. The bones, he wrapped in cloth and crushed into small pieces with a sledgehammer, just as he had done with his first victim.

He had grisly plans for the head, which he kept wrapped in a blanket for a week. The worst had been done, the nightmare came to life—what did he have left to lose? It was simply time to stop fighting his instincts, time to give into the temptations that tormented him every moment he didn't indulge them.

As an attempt to preserve the grotesque artifact—so that he could continuously use it for sexual stimulation and masturbation—he boiled it in bleach and Soilex, a type of detergent that was highly alkaline, designed to quickly dissolve the toughest greases and oils, thus making it suitable for commercial and industrial uses. Unsurprisingly, the experiment was a spectacular failure. The skull was rendered too brittle to be of any use. Like the rest of the skeleton, the skull was simply smashed into fragments and then discarded.

Everything known of Steven Tuomi's disappearance and presumed death came from Jeffrey Dahmer himself. In the eyes of the law, one could not get a more unreliable witness than a serial killer, the worst monster of them all. Even as Dahmer described the murder and subsequent disposal of the evidence with astounding detail, not one shred of evidence was found, not one fragment of Tuomi's body. Although Jeffrey candidly confessed to this particular murder in his trials, prosecutors simply could not convict him for it.

To this day, Steven Tuomi is officially classified as a missing person instead of a murder victim, and is thusly referred to as Dahmer's forgotten or lost victim.

Chapter Six:

A "Craftsman" Emerges, Perfecting the Art of Murder (Jamie Doxtator)

Steven Tuomi's murder rendered Dahmer's vicious, deadly instincts greedy and insatiable after having lain dormant for nine years.

The monster had been unleashed, and it was tempered only by what remained of Jeffrey's rational thinking. Where before, his prime concern was sating his depraved desires, this time it was evading detection. He had to be more selective with his victims; they had to be attractive, sure, but they also had to be vulnerable, lost souls nobody would miss.

James "Jamie" Doxtator fulfilled every one of those qualifications. He was a fourteen-year-old prostitute, a boy of color who spent his nights outside of gay clubs, looking for customers—one could not get a more perfect target. As if life hadn't dealt him a bad enough hand, the boy crossed paths with Jeffrey Dahmer on the night of January 16, 1988, a mere two months after Steven Tuomi suffered the same fate. They met at a bus stop just outside of 219, the same club that provided the setting for the ill-fated meeting between Dahmer and his previous victim.

Offering the boy $50 for the night, supposedly to pose nude, Dahmer brought Doxtator home with him. With neither regard nor respect for his sleeping grandmother, Dahmer engaged in oral sex with the boy and drugged him soon afterwards. His victim finally in the submissive state he preferred, Dahmer wrapped his hands around the boy's neck and strangled him to death.

His appetite for the grotesque was growing, and like a greedy child, it demanded to be indulged. More daring this time, Dahmer kept the corpse in his grandmother's basement for a week, returning to it several times to engage in necrophilia. Finally, after years of remaining only in his fantasies, death and violence met sexual desire in a deviant, macabre congregation.

When the body began to decompose, Dahmer simply disposed of it the way he had learned from his previous misdeeds. He dismembered the corpse near a floor drain, exactly as he had done with his previous victim two months before..

Chapter Seven:

Unbridled (Richard Guerrero)

D ahmer's exploits with Jamie Doxtator and his corpse could not keep the now burgeoning obsession at bay for so long. Another two months later, a new victim would meet his fate in the hands of a serial killer who was becoming better and better at the art of murder.

According to varying reports, Richard Guerrero was between the ages of twenty-one and twenty-three when he was picked up at a Milwaukee bar by Jeffrey Dahmer. As with most serial killers, a pattern was emerging. In stunning similarity to the previous victim, Guerrero was offered money in exchange for sex and was easily lured back to Dahmer's grandmother's house.

Again, after engaging in oral sex, the evolving serial killer drugged his victim by dissolving crushed sleeping pills into his drink and strangled the unconscious man to death. It was March 24, 1988.

Prone, quiet, and completely submissive, Richard lay there exactly as Jeffrey had planned, completely unaware of the torment to come. Jeffrey rested beside his victim for hours in silence, an almost peaceful air cloaking the gruesome picture. The anxieties of the living were kept at bay for a while, and Jeff once again found solace the only place he could—in death.

In keeping with his M.O., Jeff eventually dismembered the body and got rid of the remains by simply throwing them in the garbage.

For the next few months, he would retreat once again into his mind, going over the gruesome details of his crimes, revising his methods in mental preparation for the next time. It was an incubation period, the previous murder tiding him over until he could find another opportunity to enact his sick fantasies on another real, animate human being. He had gotten away with four murders so far, with nary a question about his association with his victims. He was becoming more and more audacious, growing in confidence and refining every part of his modus with every premeditated kill.

Chapter Eight:

The One That Got Away (Keison Sinthasomphone)

The story of Jeffrey Dahmer's next victim is confounding to say the least, and outrageous to most especially in retrospect.

Keison Sinthasomphone was a thirteen-year-old Laotian boy who managed to escape Jeffrey Dahmer's clutches, but while he would not end up on the growing list of murder victims, he would experience firsthand the horrors of being one of Dahmer's "chosen ones."

Jeffrey, who by this point had completely surrendered to his deviant obsessions, needed his own place, a lair in which he did not have to worry about his grandmother discovering evidence, catching him in the act, or simply growing suspicious. It would be a space all his own, where he would be free to do with his victims as he pleased. On September 25, 1988, he would move into his first apartment at 808 North 24th Street, Milwaukee, Wisconsin. A mere twenty-four hours later, he would christen the unit with another one of his crimes.

Dahmer was starved for murder, having abstained from committing one for months. Like an overexcited bloodhound, he would waste no time finding a victim.

He managed to lure the teenage Keison into his new apartment, again offering $50 to pose nude. If the boy's tender age bothered him at all, only Jeffrey would know. What is on record is how he had been able to execute the first half of his sick rituals; he drugged the boy's coffee and then fondled him soon afterwards. One can only assume that Jeffrey planned to do more, but Keison was able to escape and almost immediately report the crime to the police.

This would mark the first time Jeffrey Dahmer would be incarcerated for any of his gruesome crimes, though it bears mentioning that the punishment meted out to him was less severe than he deserved—especially for sexually assaulting a child. His lofty excuse for the unforgivable crime was that he thought the boy, who was tall for his age, was nineteen. He added that he was "an alcoholic and a homosexual with sexual problems," an admission meant to rationalize and distract from abusing a child. The police had no idea how deeply he meant those words, however, and just how dark those issues had become. Nevertheless, in January of 1989, he would be charged with second degree sexual assault and enticing a child for immoral purposes. He was released on bail one week later.

Having been promised that their son's abuser would go to prison for a long time and receive worthy punishment, Keison Sinthasomphone's parents decided not to go to court and risk exacerbating the trauma their child had already experienced. They chose instead to put their faith on the justice and legal system, a decision that they would later regret.

It would be four months before Dahmer's sentencing trial, and hard as it may be to believe, the killer wouldn't wait until then to resume his depraved activities. That he simply could not help himself, after having been incarcerated only recently, is testament to the depths of his depravity and obsession. Addicted to whatever satisfaction his murders provided, he simply could not keep the monster in shackles for very long. It had an appetite that seemed to only grow with the passage of time, becoming greedier with every indulgence. He would take his already sick activities one step further, deepening and prolonging the pleasure he took from them by conducting "experiments" and collecting trophies.

On Easter Sunday, March 25, 1989, a day after the secret anniversary of Richard Guerrero's death, Jeffrey Dahmer would claim his fifth murder victim.

Chapter Nine:

Easter Impudence (Anthony Sears)

Anthony Sears was a 26-year-old bisexual man, an aspiring model who fit Jeffrey's particular type to a T. He was African-American, lean, attractive, and accepting of Dahmer's advances. Though he had a girlfriend at the time, Sears was more than happy to flirt with and entertain the young man with the boyish good looks.

The setting, a Milwaukee gay club called *La Cage,* was dark. The alcohol was cold, and the conversation was stimulating. It was one of those nights that promised possibilities, the seduction of a few alcohol-fueled hours and the simulation of friendship too formidable to resist.

The night wore on, and when the conversation outlived opening hours, Dahmer and Sears decided to continue the party elsewhere. They were with two other men, Sears' friends Bob Keel and Jeffrey Connor, who drove the couple to Dahmer's grandmother's house. Dahmer must have orchestrated this, aware of the possibility that police might be surveilling his apartment thanks to his current legal predicament.

Dropping them off at an intersection just a bit farther north of the house in West Allis (Dahmer was savvy enough to have given them a fake address, so that they would not have an actual location to give to police later on), Connor told Sears to call if he needed a ride back home, reminding the latter that he was going to be spending Easter with his family and that he was having lunch with his mother. Little did Keel and Connor know that it would be the last time they saw their friend.

Having gained some privacy, Dahmer and Sears walked to his grandmother's house, entering through the white side door and proceeding down the stairs. The two engaged in intercourse that night. Afterwards, a drugged drink would put Sears to sleep, rendering him submissive to his captor in an unconscious state. Alike to his previous murders, Dahmer would then progress to strangle the young man to death and subsequently dismember him. This time, however, he would indulge in more of his debauched curiosities.

He set aside the head and the genitals to mummify and preserve later, disposing the rest of the body in the way to which he had grown accustomed. Fascinated by Sears' ponytail, he scalped the head before boiling and skinning it. He kept the skull as a memento and was so captivated by it that for days after, he would take it to work and stare at it during his breaks. Years later, in a black cabinet, it would be found amongst his belongings, painted red.

Anthony's mother, Marilyn Sears, was going to see her son the next day to celebrate the latter's recent job promotion; he had a new position as manager at a Baker's Square restaurant. Marilyn was troubled by her only son standing her up for Easter dinner, hoping that he had simply left town and for one reason or another was unable to let her know. After all, while things were going well for him, he had expressed that he wanted to leave Milwaukee. When he never got in touch with her, Marilyn reported his disappearance to the police. Unfortunately, nothing would come of this report.

In an interview years later, Dahmer would describe Sears as "exceptionally attractive," and further articulate, "If I could've kept him longer, all of him, I would have." Of course, it did not occur to Jeffrey that he actually *could* have, had he kept Sears as a living, breathing friend rather than an inanimate, fragmented memento.

On May 23, 1989, months after he was released on bail, Dahmer was sentenced for the crimes he committed against the teenage Keison Sinthasomphone. Citing his poor excuses—that he thought Keison was nineteen, and that he was merely a troubled gay man—Dahmer pleaded for leniency, which would be granted to him. He was sentenced to five years for sexual assault and three years for enticing a child for immoral purposes, to be served concurrently. He would only serve ten months in a workers' release program, forcing him to move out of his first apartment, and five years' probation. It was a slap on the wrist, and still no one knew the magnitude of his depravity. He was continuing to escape true justice, and the rest of his crimes would not come to light until more victims met their fate by his hands.

Because the Sinthasomphone family never went to court, only Keison ever recognized what Jeffrey Dahmer looked like..

Chapter Ten:

A Housewarming (Raymond Smith)

Eight months into serving his sentence in a work camp, Dahmer moved into a new residence in downtown Milwaukee, the now infamous Apartment 213 on North 25ᵗʰ street. Here, he would violently slaughter and desecrate the bodies of the majority of his victims. It would remain as his last lair of bloodshed.

Astonishingly, his most recent brush with the legal system would not deter him from resuming his crimes and even escalating the gruesomeness of his rituals; and on May 29, 1990, a mere two weeks after Dahmer had moved in, Raymond Lamont Smith aka Ricky Beeks, would become his sixth known murder victim and the first to experience many of his aggressor's new rituals.

Smith a thirty-three year old at the time met Jeffrey at Club 219, making him older than most of his typical victims. Dahmer, worked his charm—or expertise at manipulation, depending on how one perceived it—and managed to convince the his new companion to come home with him for a night of "entertainment."

In a dark christening of his new apartment, Dahmer put seven sleeping pills into Raymond Smith's drink, before choking him. He had slightly altered his pattern at this point by killing the victim before obtaining any sexual pleasure; he performed oral sex with Raymond Smith's corpse, finally crossing over into the realm of necrophilia, one of the most taboo sexual inclinations known to society.

After violating his new victim's corpse in the vilest of ways, he realized that he wanted to prolong the "high" this murder provided him, and he purchased a Polaroid camera the very next day. It would be with this camera that he would take the pictures that investigators later discovered.

He fashioned Smith's body into several suggestive positions, and began to snap photographs of the cadaver as it lay limp and lifeless. Only once Dahmer was satisfied with the pictures he took did he place the body in the bathtub to be dismembered. As he had done many times before, he boiled several of the body parts—the arms, pelvis, and legs—in Soilex, and dissolved the remainder of the corpse in acid. He would later paint Raymond Smith's skull gray and arranged it beside Anthony Sears' in a black cabinet. Some of the other bones were displayed as decorations around his apartment.

This murder would mark Jeffrey Dahmer's indulgence in true necrophilia. As he would later admit, it was the first time he had actually had sex with a dead body

Chapter Eleven:

The Anomaly (Edward Smith)

Dahmer would not wait months to claim his next victim. The last of his inhibitions had gone with the murder of Raymond Smith. As a testament to this new level of boldness, his next victim would not exactly fit the profile of the previous ones.

Edward "Eddie" Smith, known in his social circle simply as "Sheikh," was actually a friend of Jeffrey's. People who knew him described Eddie as the "life of the party," a kind, outgoing man who was well loved and easy to get along with. He was last seen on the night of June 14, 1990, when he left the Phoenix Bar, another local joint in Milwaukee.

Unlike the other victims, Eddie had been to Dahmer's apartment several times without incident, and to anyone who had observed them together, they seemed to have a good, easygoing friendship. But of course, no one yet knew of the evils that lurked in Jeffrey Dahmer's mind.

It is unclear if the killer had been fantasizing or pondering the murder of his friend long before the act itself. Had it been that first time he met the twenty-eight-year-old Eddie in another bar? Did he form the thoughts at one of their hang-out sessions at Apartment 213? What stopped him all those other times? Fear of discovery? Circumstance? Or had he developed a genuine friendship?

Perhaps it was simply a decision he'd made in the moment, an alcohol-fueled verdict. Only Dahmer could ever really have known.

It can only be assumed that on the night of his death, Eddie had no idea that a visit to his friend would not exactly be a social call. The man he trusted would drug his drink, strangle him to death, and then use his corpse to explore and indulge in twisted curiosities.

Wanting to experiment with another method of preservation, Dahmer used a knife to remove Eddie's flesh, and then put the skeleton in the freezer, hoping that freezing it would also remove the moisture. He stored the carcass for months, his efforts ultimately ending in disappointment. While he dissolved the bones in acid to finally get rid of the evidence, he would try once more to preserve the skull. Transferring the skull from the freezer straight into an oven, where it eventually burst. To Dahmer, the only "saving grace" of this experimental project was that he was able to take pictures of some parts of the process.

Later, the serial killer would explain, "I felt rotten about Smith's murder as I was unable to retain any parts of his body."

Chapter Twelve:

The Cannibal Rises (Ernest Miller)

I nstead of another bar or club, it was on the street in front of a bookstore that Dahmer met Ernest Miller on September 2, 1990. The dashing twenty-four-year-old dancer was also offered money in exchange for sex and a good time. Known to have a charming, almost smug confidence about him, Miller could not have guessed what his acquiescence would lead to.

In a retrospectively unsettling anecdote, Dahmer recalled that the young man had allowed him to listen to his heartbeat and the soft rumbling of his stomach, but when the killer tried to perform oral sex on his would-be victim, the cheeky Ernest Miller stopped him, saying, "That will cost you extra."

The small act of protest would prove to be of no consequence to Dahmer, who would put two sleeping pills in Miller's drink in an attempt to knock him out. He typically used three, however he had run out of the drug and it was all he had left. The dosage was not enough to put Miller down for very long. He would awaken much sooner than expected, and Dahmer would be forced to alter his pattern. Instead of strangling his companion, a panicked Dahmer snatched a knife, slit Miller's throat, and observed as he bled to death. It would only take a few minutes, but he used the time to take pictures as Miller lay on the carpet, fading away.

Now that his prey was unable to reject him, Dahmer snapped more pictures of the corpse with his Polaroid camera, once again positioning the body in suggestive poses. He conversed with his now unresponsive companion and occasionally planted kisses on the still handsome face.

Dahmer also altered his method of disposal this time. He set aside Miller's biceps, heart, and slices of the legs, deciding to save them later for another nefarious act—cannibalism. He kept these portions of human meat in his freezer for later consumption. He once again attempted preservation of the full skeleton by separating flesh and bone, and then treating the latter with a light bleach solution. Dahmer would then hang the bleached skeleton in a wardrobe. The skull, he gifted particular attention to. Just as he had with the two previous victims, Jeffrey painted the skull and then covered it in an enamel coating

Chapter Thirteen:

Not His Type
(David Thomas)

The month would not end before Jeffrey Dahmer struck again. On September 24, 1990, a mere three weeks after his last murder, Dahmer would strike up a conversation with the twenty-two-year-old David Thomas. Located at The Grand Avenue Mall, a local shopping center, Thomas who had been dropped off by his relatives, hit it off with Dahmer.

Jeffrey was an expert at this point, and he managed to convince the unwitting stranger to come back to his apartment. Dahmer presumably offered money for Thomas to pose for nude pictures, as he had done several times before.

Once back at his "lair," Dahmer had full intentions of doing to Thomas what he had done to all the hapless young men that had come before him. A drink laced with the killer's drug of preference, and his ninth victim would fall predictably unconscious. An unexpected conundrum faced Dahmer at this point—he realized that Thomas wasn't his type, and the young man just didn't seem as attractive anymore now that he was unconscious.

But it was too late to turn back now. If he let Thomas go, the latter would surely know he had been drugged. Dahmer would be risking retaliation from his victim, and more significantly exposure. This would just not do, of course. He had big plans yet for his future victims. There was so much still to be explored, to be tested, no matter how macabre the methodology.

Ultimately, the selfishness won out. It seemed that Dahmer had lost whatever human empathy he'd possessed a long time ago. David Thomas would end up strangled and dead at the hands of Jeffrey Dahmer. He would be the first victim Dahmer killed purely out of necessity instead of sexual attraction.

Not wanting to waste his efforts, Dahmer continued his process and took many photographs of the body at different stages of the dismemberment—before, during, and after. Video footage might even have existed, though it was never confirmed. He was beginning to consider the process of murder and disposal an art, after all, and despite the less than ideal victim, he could still find some pleasure in the situation.

It would be with the many Polaroids that David's sister would later identify her missing brother. As Dahmer was uninterested in keeping around any part of Thomas' cadaver, he disposed of the entire corpse, and none of the remains were ever found. The assumption is that, like many of the other victims, the body (or parts of it) was dissolved in acid and flushed down the toilet.

David's loved ones would have a very different opinion as to what his life was worth, but whether or not Dahmer gave this even a passing thought remains a mystery. What makes David's story even more heartbreaking is just how much he meant to the people in his life. He had a girlfriend and two children, and he had been raised in a close-knit family, one that had a habit of updating each other on important life events. They always knew each member of the families whereabouts—especially if they were going on trips—because they phoned each other frequently, so when David disappeared, the worry almost immediately began nagging at the back of their minds.

Perhaps he'd had a disagreement with someone in the family, or had to take care of something privately? They also knew that he wanted to pursue a career in rap; could the opportunity of a lifetime have come up? An opportunity so sudden that he hadn't yet found a minute to give them a call? Perhaps he had to leave town and was meaning to pick up the phone the second he got the chance...

They rationalized his disappearance at first, not wanting to panic or entertain darker thoughts. The denial held on by a fragile thread, however, because it could not have been more unlike David to just up and disappear without telling any of his relatives. Tragically, the Thomas family would not find out what happened to David until Jeffrey Dahmer's confessions in 1991. Until then, they simply had to bear the sleepless nights.

During the trial more than a year later, Inez Thomas, David's mother, looked right at her son's killer and let him know exactly how he had impacted her life. "That was my baby boy you took away from me," she said. In response, Jeffrey Dahmer simply kept silent, his eyes on the floor

Chapter Fourteen:

A Trail of Blood

Curtis Straughter

Dahmer would be unable to claim another human being's life for almost five months after David Thomas' death. This was not, however, for lack of trying. According to reports, he failed at acquiring a victim five times in that period.

On February 18, 1991, a rainy Monday, Jeffrey watched a nineteen-year-old waiting patiently at a bus stop near Marquette University. A member of Gay Youth Milwaukee, aspiring model Curtis Durrell Straughter often referred to himself by the moniker Demetra. Aside from his would-be killer, it was his grandmother who last saw him.

Curtis was a high school dropout. He had recently been terminated from his job as a nursing aide. His future was hazy at best, but it was not unlike the experience of a lot of people his age. Nevertheless, the uncertainty and aimlessness were sources of anxiety, and Dahmer, like a shark smelling blood, gravitated towards those conditions.

Dahmer had become adept at convincing his victims to go with him willingly, and without much hesitation, he simply approached Straughter at the bus stop and struck up a conversation. Companionship, validation, and possibly sex—what Dahmer represented was a welcome respite not just from the bad weather, but also from the recent worries of Straughter's life.

Acquiring the boy's trust would not be a difficult task for Dahmer. Offering $50 for nude photos, Dahmer managed to lure Curtis to Apartment 213, where he would strangle the young man with a leather belt as the latter was giving him oral sex. Curtis would be the only victim Dahmer didn't first sedate with drugs. Instead, Dahmer had handcuffed him, rendering him virtually helpless. The boy was fully conscious when the killer strangled him to death.

In the bathtub, he expertly cut up Curtis' body, documenting the process by taking several photos with his Polaroid camera. He disposed of everything but the skull, hands, and genitals, which he would preserve. He crushed the bones, and simply threw the rest of the body parts in the garbage. He kept the skull as a souvenir, but unlike Anthony Sears' and Ernest Miller's, he left it unpainted.

Curtis Straughter was Dahmer's tenth murder victim. Whether the killer was keeping count was unclear, but at this point, it's easy to assume that he had completely lost touch of seeing his victims as human beings, individuals who were precious to someone.

Curtis' mother Dorothy would remind the world of these young men's value during the trial later on. In her victim impact statement, she would say that she had "a lot of hatred, a lot of anger." She tells the court how, for over a year, she had not seen nor heard from her son, and that now she never would. In response, Jeffrey Dahmer would merely keep his eyes lowered, showing neither remorse nor any other emotion.

Errol Lindsey

A little less than two months later, on April 7, 1991, nineteen-year-old Errol Lindsey went shopping at The Grand Avenue. Lindsey was a choir member at the Greater Spring Hill Missionary Baptist Church, where he was known to be a charming, easily liked young man with a wide, ready smile for everybody.

After shopping that fateful Sunday in 1991, he went back to his mother's apartment on 24th Street and stepped out again to have a key made. It was by pure circumstance that he would pass by 27th and Kilbourn. What exactly drew him there is unclear, but it's possible that a boombox was to blame. Lindsey was a fan of rap music, and someone was playing it pretty loudly.

There, Dahmer met the nineteen-year-old Errol Lindsey outside of a bookstore—a mere two blocks from Apartment 213. This was the same spot from which Dahmer had picked up Ernest Miller in September of the previous year. The young Lindsey had no clue that he would suffer the same fate.

Unlike the previous victims, Errol Lindsey was not a homosexual. Nevertheless, Jeffrey was able to convince the young man to go with him—again, with the promise of $50 for nude pictures.

The killer had another experiment he wanted to perform. Rather than killing Lindsey, he wanted to turn the nineteen-year-old into a type of zombie, a submissive companion with neither free will nor any sentience. After serving Lindsey with a drink heavily laced with a sedative, Dahmer brought out his tools. He used a power drill to create a hole in Lindsey's skull through which he poured muriatic acid. Unexpectedly, Lindsey was startled awake, presumably by the sound of the drill, and it soon became obvious that despite being groggy from the sedatives he'd been given, he was no zombie. He was lucid enough to have a fairly firm grasp of the situation—he knew where he was and whose apartment it belonged to. He said, "I have a headache. What time is it?" Dahmer responded with disproportionate violence.

In a fit of frustration and disappointment, Dahmer drugged the boy again and then murdered him the same way he had murdered the others. He strangled Lindsey, had sexual relations with the corpse, and then decapitated him. He then flayed the corpse and continued to brine the skin in a mixture of salt and cold water in another attempt at preservation. This would be another failed experiment, however, and the remains would later decompose. After a few weeks he would submerge the remains in acid. While he disposed of the rest of the body, keeping the skull as a souvenir.

At Dahmer's much publicized trial, Lindsey's sister would gain notoriety for attempting to attack her brother's killer, shouting "I hate you, Jeffrey!" among other profanities. She was a petite woman, but it took five strong officers to restrain her.

Anthony "Tony" Hughes

The murder of Tony Hughes would illustrate just how cold and detached from any human empathy Dahmer had become. Tony didn't fit the profile of the killer's preferred victim. At thirty-one, Tony was older than most of Dahmer's victims, but that wasn't what made him unique. The man was both deaf and mute, lending him a different sort of vulnerability than Dahmer was used to.

Some reports say that he and Dahmer had been exchanging letters for either a few weeks or years before Hughes' death, and the murderer would later claim that they had a relationship, but it is unclear if this was ever verified. Perhaps this was simply a friendship that Dahmer could not stand to lose, sealing Tony's grisly fate.

It was May 24, and Hughes was only in town that Sunday to visit his family, having moved to Madison the year before. Wanting to make the most out of the trip, he informed his relatives that he would be going out to see some of his friends, but that he would be back shortly.

It was by chance that Dahmer ran into Hughes outside of a establishment called 219 Club. They engaged in the pleasant conversation that was essential to Dahmer's modus. Hughes read lips, and his companion wrote down responses. Aided by hand signals, they were able to have a good time, and Dahmer eventually set his plan, which by now had become routine, in motion.

$50 for nude pictures, the promise of a quiet night watching videos, and easily acquired trust brought Anthony Hughes to Apartment 213, where his so-called "friend" gave him a drink spiked with sleeping pills. This time, Dahmer would not have sex with his victim; whether the reasons were benevolent or not, only Dahmer could really know. It's a thought that's difficult to swallow because what Dahmer *did* plan to do was no act of kindness or compassion.

Once Tony was unconscious, Dahmer attempted yet again to create a subservient zombie. The killer drilled a small hole into his companion's skull and then injected the cranial cavity with acid. Dahmer waited in anticipation, hoping that when Tony woke up, he would finally have the perfect companion. Alas, Tony would never wake up, much less fulfill Dahmer's sick, perverted fantasy.

The reasons are unclear, but Dahmer did not immediately dismember or dispose of Hughes' body. Perhaps he would once again indulge in necrophilia, or he simply wanted to prolong the thrill of his most recent kill. The corpse would stay in his bed for several days before being dismembered and dissolved in acid, exclusive of the skull, which Dahmer would add to his collection of mementos.

Chapter Fifteen:

The Brother (Konerak Sinthasomphone)

Lightning would strike twice for one of the families of Dahmer's victims, this time with worse consequences. If Keison Sinthasomphone's story was a miscarriage of justice, his younger brother Konerak's would be a grim illustration of downright incompetence, and possibly even racism, within the legal system.

It had been almost three years since Keison miraculously escaped the clutches of one of the worst serial killers the world had yet to discover. He had been molested, and while Dahmer was incarcerated and served time for the crime, the rest of the Sinthasomphone family would never know what Keison's assaulter looked like. They would never even be informed of Dahmer's early release.

Keison was thirteen when he was abused by Dahmer; his brother Konerak would be fourteen upon meeting the same man. Perhaps Konerak's familiar features drew Dahmer to him; did the boy remind the killer of the one that got away? Did he see Keison in the same lithe, lean features? The color of his skin? Or perhaps the boy simply fit

Dahmer's victim profile; Konerak was young, good-looking, vulnerable, and a person of color.

They met at a place where Dahmer had hunted before—the Grand Avenue Mall. It was May 27, 1991, a mere three days after the murder of Anthony Hughes. It was by pure chance that murderer and victim would meet that day. Dahmer made his usual offer of $50 for nude photos, but it would not be an easy sell this time. Konerak was rightfully hesitant to go with a stranger; whether or not this was because of what happened with his brother years earlier is unclear. Eventually, however, Dahmer's expertise won out, and the monster was able to convince Konerak to leave with him.

At Apartment 213, where in the bedroom Tony Hughes body still lay, the boy stripped down to his underwear and posed for photos. When Dahmer was satisfied with his shots, he drugged the fourteen-year-old and brought out his drill.

Having been disappointed with how his experiment with his previous victim turned out, Dahmer was eager to try again. He justified his failure by blaming it on a "bad drilling technique," so with more caution this time, he created a small hole in Konerak's skull and injected acid into the frontal lobe.

Amazingly, the teen actually woke up, though he was obviously woozy and disoriented from both the sedatives and the acid already damaging a part of his brain. Dahmer brought the new "zombie" to the bedroom, not caring that Tony's body was on display. Too dazed and groggy from the drugs and the acid, Konerak did not react to the sight of the corpse.

The boy passed out again, and Dahmer took the opportunity to revel in his momentary success. He lay beside the teen and drank beer as he pondered his current situation. How long would his new zombie last this time? What else could he do to indulge in his seemingly insatiable appetites?

As a testament to how complacent he had become after so many murders (and getting away with them), Dahmer went out to purchase more beer, leaving an unconscious Konerak with the corpse in his bedroom.

Hard as it may be to believe, considering he was still pumped with a high dosage of drugs and was now suffering brain damage from having acid being poured into his skull, Konerak managed to wake up. Naked and disoriented, he managed to stumble out of the apartment and onto the street. He unfortunately would not make it very far. Dahmer would return to find his victim surrounded by three of his neighbors. Unconvinced with Dahmer's explanations that the boy was his lover and that he was simply drunk, the women remained concerned and skeptical. It was when Dahmer described the teen's behavior as "normal" and began ushering him back into the apartment that the women informed their neighbor that they had already called 911.

The police were on their way, but Dahmer remained calm. With the news of the police on their way Jeffrey had time to get his bearings and polish his lie. By the time officers Joseph Gabrish and John Balcerzak arrived, Dahmer was composed, and unruffled. He told the men what he had told his neighbors, who were still standing there in disbelief. The women tried to tell the officers that something wasn't right, especially because they had noticed how Konerak seemed to be physically trying to escape from Dahmer's clutch. They were told by the officers to "butt out," "shut the hell up," and not to interfere. At this point, it seemed that they were already convinced by the word of a white male adult that this was a domestic issue.

To cement his credibility, Dahmer retrieved from his apartment the suggestive pictures he had taken of Konerak not long before, and showed them to the officers, who merely stretched their necks a bit to peek into the unit. Despite the strange odor clearly coming from inside, the policemen did not find it prudent to investigate any further. "Take good care of him," they told Dahmer, leaving Konerak's fate back in the killer's hands.

Had they simply listened to the alarm bells ringing and indulged their professional curiosity, they would have found Tony Hughes' body in the bedroom and human remains all over the apartment, some in plain sight and being used as décor. They might even have realized that Konerak was not an adult but a fourteen-year-old child whose older brother had been victimized by the same man years before. There would have been more than enough evidence of Dahmer's heinous crimes and in turn ending his killing spree right then and there.

Unfortunately, the officers would leave happy with their judgement, and Konerak would soon suffer a terrible fate shortly after.

Dahmer was displeased with what had just happened. It seemed that his "zombie" just wasn't "zombie" enough after all, if the boy still had the wherewithal to attempt an escape and even try to physically pull away from his attacker.

Wondering if he could still salvage the situation, Dahmer took some more hydrochloric acid and injected the substance into Konerak's brain. This time, the boy would never wake up. No death went to waste with Dahmer, however, and the killer indulged once again in necrophiliac acts.

He now had two corpses in his apartment, and the encounter with the police officers was too close a call to ignore, so Dahmer skipped work the next day to get rid of the bodies. In accordance with the methodology he had painstakingly developed, he cut up the bodies and liquefied them with acid. The skulls, as usual he kept as souvenirs

Chapter Sixteen:

The Last Leg

Dahmer had killed four people so far that year, and he would kill another four before 1991 was over. His killing spree had truly kicked in at this point, and he was no longer waiting long periods of time before taking another victim.

Matt Turner

If there ever was a young man in his prime, it was Matt Turner. He was a flamboyant, adventurous twenty-year-old who was known as the life of the party, someone who had the uncanny ability to make friends anywhere and everywhere. His affable, bubbly personality served him well at his job bussing tables at a pizzeria. As his alter-ego Donald Montrell, he also lip-synced at a local bar, indulging his love for dressing up, getting photographed, and being the center of attention. People who knew him—friends, customers, and employers— remembered him fondly as an independent, fun-loving young man who always had a ready smile.

He would display this gift for easy socializing on June 30, 1991, at the Chicago Gay Pride parade that Dahmer had also attended. The young man was hard to miss, and amidst the colorful costumes and impassioned cheering, Dahmer groomed his fourteenth victim. He propositioned the unassuming Matt with money in exchange for photographs, and because the latter liked to pose for pictures anyway, it's likely what convinced him to get on a Greyhound bus with Dahmer. They went back to Milwaukee together, the younger man oblivious to the fact that he would never leave.

At Apartment 213, Matt would meet the same fate as too many other young men. Dahmer would drug, strangle, and dismember him. In a fifty-seven-gallon drum, the killer submerged Matt's body in acid, except for some of the select organs, which he stored in the freezer and intended to consume later. He also kept the skull as a keepsake.

Matt's family would not immediately be alarmed by his disappearance. They were used to the young man leaving without prior notice and not being heard from for long periods of time. Matt had been born with one foot out the door, so to speak, and he was always meeting people and trying new things. This time, however, Matt would never return.

Jeremiah "Jeremy" Weinberger

The story of Dahmer's fifteenth victim has one of the saddest endings brought about by the killer's actions. Two lives would meet an abrupt end as a consequence of Jeffrey Dahmer's sick obsessions.

Jeremy Weinberger was known to everyone as a sweet and trusting young man. He was highly regarded among his friends, who faulted him only for being "a little naive." Even Dahmer would remember him fondly, saying of him, "He was exceptionally affectionate. He was nice to be with."

On July 6, 1991, they met in Chicago, where the twenty-three-year-old half Puerto Rican worked as a customer service representative. Ninety miles away from Milwaukee, a bar called Carol Speakeasy would be where their fates crossed. Naturally personable, it was not difficult for Dahmer to lure the young man into a conversation that by all accounts seemed perfectly normal and casual. Dahmer invited Jeremy to leave with him to Milwaukee. Considering the interesting, exciting proposition, Jeremy asked a friend what his opinion was of Dahmer. "Seems fine," the friend replied. Having received a stamp of approval, Jeremy got on a bus and left with Dahmer.

Upon arriving in Milwaukee, Dahmer would not immediately kill his new victim. So charmed was he with Jeremy that the pair spent a few days together. But of course, this almost blissful period had to come to an end, and Jeremy decided it was time for him to return home. The overwhelming fear of being abandoned once again engulfed Dahmer. If it was time for his prey to leave, then it was time to kill him.

Offering one last drink to the young man, Dahmer drugged him with sedatives and waited until he lost consciousness. Attempting once again to create a "zombie" out of yet another human being he wanted to possess and dominate, Dahmer drilled a hole into Jeremy's skull, and this time, instead of using acid, he injected boiling water into the brain.

Miraculously, the young man would wake up from this experiment with no substantial signs of zombification. It wasn't too late to try again, however, so Dahmer drugged him for the second time and injected the brain with another dose of boiling water. This time, Jeremy would fall into a two-day coma, after which Dahmer would come home to find him dead with his eyes open.

Another disappointment meant another execution of the ritual of disposal. Dahmer cut the body into pieces and stored the head in his freezer.

Later, when the murders came to light, the tragedy would result in another. Jeremy's friend, the very same one who gave him the green light to go with Dahmer and watched them leave together, would fall into a deep depression borne out of misplaced guilt. He would slit his wrists and walk to a friend's house as he bled. He would die in that same friend's arms.

Oliver Lacy

Unperturbed by the death of a kind, sweet young man with his life ahead of him, Dahmer would go on to kill a several more unsuspecting innocents.

Victim No. 16 was Oliver Lacy, a twenty-three-year-old father to a two-year-old. He had moved to Milwaukee to be with his new family and was about to propose to his girlfriend.

Killer and victim would meet on the same day the former was terminated from his job at Ambrosia Chocolate Co. By this point, Dahmer was drinking heavily and letting himself go, consumed with one thing, and on thing only: finding a young man to experiment with and turn into his personal zombie.

Oliver was last seen on July 12, 1991 at the Grand Avenue Mall, an old hunting ground for Jeffrey Dahmer. Though Oliver seemed to have much in his life going for him at that point in time, he somehow agreed to go back to Apartment 213 and pose for nude photos in exchange for the usual $50 Dahmer offered. There, Lacy would meet the same fate as the young men who had fallen for the murderer's seemingly normal countenance. He would be drugged, strangled, and sexually assaulted. In another display of curiosity, Dahmer would try to use chloroform to render his victim unconscious before failing and simply reverting to his usual method of strangling.

Dahmer sodomized the corpse before dismembering it, taking pictures along the way. He stored Lacy's head in the refrigerator, placing it beside a container of Arm and Hammer baking soda in an attempt to mitigate the odor. Planning to consume it later, he also plastic-wrapped the heart. He kept the rest of the skeleton in his freezer.

Oliver Lacy would be the very first victim to be identified by the authorities, as he had the most remains found in the apartment.

An article published on August 24, 1991 recounts a memorial service held at the Lively Stone Missionary Baptist Church. Oliver was fondly called "Birdie" by his family. During the service, they tried to focus on the joyful aspects of Birdie's life, instead of his untimely, tragic, gruesome demise. His killer, after all, was already receiving all the publicity and attention, and they refused to entitle him to more of the same.

Birdie was an athlete. In 1987, he was part of the Oak Park-River Forest High School's state championship team as a sprinter. His energy transcended sports as well, and he was known to be energetic and a lover of life. Madis Lacy, his aunt, would say of him, "I think the thing I will miss most about Birdie was his smile. He never let anything get him down."

Joseph Bradehoft

At twenty-five, Joseph Bradehoft was already a father of three children. His pending divorce drove him to Milwaukee, where he attempted to find work in order to provide for his children. His brother Donald lived there, and Joseph was looking forward to spending time with family as well.

It was raining on July 19, 1991 when the young man found himself holding a pack of beer at a bus stop. This is where Jeffrey Dahmer would approach him and offer him $50 for a few pictures and a good time. The weather was bad, and he could use the cash, so Joseph willingly went with the stranger to Apartment 213, where he would meet his demise.

Jeffrey crushed drugs into his new guest's drink, waited for the sedatives to kick in, and then strangled the young man to death. For days, he would continue to sexually abuse the corpse, covering it with a sheet in his bed. A maggot infestation in the head would force him to finally start the process of disposal.

Jeffrey dismembered the body, cleaning out the head and placing it in the freezer. In a fifty-seven-gallon blue tub of acid, Bradehoft's torso would join two others.

Unbeknownst to Jeffrey, he was nearing the end of his gruesome killing spree. Joseph Bradehoft would be his seventeenth and final victim

Chapter Seventeen:

The Anti-Hero
(Tracy Edwards)

Tracy Edwards, who was no stranger to a life of crime himself, would be hailed as the unexpected hero that escaped and put away the Milwaukee Cannibal.

He met the murderer at another bar in Milwaukee. Perhaps Dahmer could sense that Edwards would not be as easy to lure as the other victims, so he sweetened his usual proposition of $50. He offered Edwards $100 instead to pose for photographs. The young man took the bait and decided to spend the night with the friendly stranger.

A strong, odd odor immediately greeted Edwards as they arrived at Apartment 213. There stood a large blue drum and boxes of acid strewn about the living room. "They're used for cleaning tiles," Dahmer casually explained.

On the television, a popular horror film was playing— one of The Exorcist movies. The situation was getting stranger by the minute, and Edwards' senses sparked into high alert. He was calmed somewhat by the casual conversation that commenced, though this sense of security would be short-lived.

Dahmer distracted Edwards by bringing attention to the tropical fish tank in the room. At the flick of a switch, the soft-spoken, friendly man turned into the manic, deranged killer. When Edwards turned to view the tank, Dahmer caught the man's right wrist with the handcuffs he had been secretly holding. Edwards was quick to pull away, however, and the killer would fail to handcuff the other wrist.

Failing to restrain his victim, Dahmer brought out a six-inch knife, telling his victim in no uncertain terms that he would photograph him naked, carve his heart out, and then eat it. Edwards would later recount how he witnessed the killer display strange behaviors like rocking back and forth and muttering something under his breath as his eyes remained on the television screen, mesmerized by the disturbing scenes in The Exorcist.

In an attempt to calm him down, Tracy began to unbutton his shirt, repeatedly placating the killer by saying that they were friends and that there was no need for the knife. The desire for survival was strong, and as he tried to appease Dahmer, he waited for an opportunity to escape.

Noticing that the strange man was no longer holding the knife, Edwards lunged and hit Dahmer on the side of his head. The handcuffs still hanging from his wrist, Tracy ran out of the apartment at around half an hour before midnight.

At the corner of Kilbourn Avenue and 25th street, Officer Mueller and Officer Rauth were in a patrol car when they noticed "a man frantically running down the street in handcuffs." Thinking that he might have been escaping another officer, they immediately stopped the man, who was actually flagging them down. Edwards blurted out the terrifying events of his night, telling them that a crazy "freak" handcuffed him and threatened to eat his heart.

Together, the three of them went back to Apartment 213, where a prepared Dahmer had switched back to his "nice guy" persona. Calmly, he invited the group inside and admitted that he had put handcuffs on Edwards. When asked for an explanation, however, he could not give one.

Officer Mueller made for the bedroom to retrieve the knife Edwards said he would probably find there. Dahmer attempted to overtake the policeman and keep him from finding whatever was in the room, but Officer Rauth stopped him, telling him sternly to "back off." Having run out of luck, Dahmer had no choice but to do as he was told.

In the bedroom, Officer Mueller indeed found the knife on the bedside table, but what truly caught his attention were the disturbing Polaroids in the open drawer. He could hardly believe his eyes; the images featured human bodies in different stages of dismemberment and deterioration, limbs contorted into unnatural angles. There were more than a dozen of these pictures in the pile, and flipping through them, Mueller recognized the very same apartment they were in. "These are for real," he mumbled to his partner in disbelief.

Whatever was left of Dahmer's composure disappeared, and he lunged after the policemen, who easily restrained him. Moments later, the killer would be held down on the floor, bounded by handcuffs. The situation was eerily similar to what Tracy Edwards narrowly escaped from earlier that night.

The officers called for backup, and Mueller proceeded to search the rest of the apartment. It wasn't long before he was standing before Jeffrey's refrigerator. The cool air hit his face at the same time his eyes landed on a human head staring right back at him. He heard a scream then, not immediately realizing that it was his own. "There's a f****** head in the refrigerator!" he yelled.

Still immobilized on the floor, a resigned Dahmer replied, "For what I did, I should be dead."

It did not take long for the shocking discovery to reach public circulation. News outlets painted Tracy Edwards as the hero that ended the Milwaukee Cannibal's killing spree. "He underestimated me. God sent me there to take care of the situation," Edwards said, enjoying the positive attention. His time in the limelight would be short-lived, however, as the publicity led to the State of Mississippi being able to find him and subsequently issue a warrant of arrest. Edwards was soon extradited to Mississippi to face the consequences of a crime he himself had committed—sexually assaulting a fourteen-year-old girl.

When Edwards later returned to Milwaukee, he sued the city's police department for five million dollars on the basis that they did not take seriously the complaints the neighbors of Dahmer made regarding his strange behavior and the foul odor coming from Apartment 213. Had they investigated more thoroughly, the killer's crimes would have come to light earlier; lives could have been saved, and Edwards would not have had to experience the trauma of almost being one of his victims. Nothing would ever come of this lawsuit as it would be thrown out almost immediately.

Later, Tracy Edwards would not receive a share of the restitution from Dahmer's estate along with the other victims' families. Edwards would receive no compensation for his ordeal, aside from his five minutes of fame as the man who vanquished the Milwaukee Monster.

Though Dahmer is not entirely to blame for Edwards' personal troubles, those who knew the latter did state that the events that happened in Apartment 213 certainly contributed to his downward spiral. His drug and alcohol addictions were exacerbated, placing him in prison several times throughout his life. When he wasn't in prison, he was roaming the streets, homeless and jumping from shelter to shelter.

Years later, Tracy would serve time for his participation in the drowning of another homeless man. He was one of two people seen to be arguing with the victim. His lawyer used his trauma in relation to the infamous Jeffrey Dahmer as his defense

Chapter Eighteen:

Apartment 213, a Museum of Horror

Jeffrey Dahmer's infamous lair was filled with knick-knacks too grotesque for the average person's imagination. Investigators would find a wealth of evidence in that small, dingy apartment that became the laboratory and playground of one of the most notorious serial killers ever to have been exposed.

As strange as it sounds, it seemed that Dahmer had made the place his own version of home. The living room was filled with décor, some of it nothing out of the ordinary. Others, however, took on a darker meaning once his crimes came to light.

In the living room, there were indoor plants and a fish tank. Later, investigators would discover that aside from his unplugged freezer, Dahmer used the fish tank as a prop to explain the putrid odors coming from his apartment. On the walls hung artworks of nude men in provocative positions, a startling echo of what would be portrayed in the Polaroids Dahmer took himself.

Another oddity found in the apartment enlightened investigators that the man was not done "decorating." They found a sketch of what appeared to be the altar or shrine Dahmer was planning to build using lamps, light bulbs, incense, a black and white carpet, a black chair, and human bones from his personal collection. At the very center would be a black table on top of which were painted skulls. On the same piece of paper were notes for the colors and materials he wanted to use.

Dahmer would later confess that on the same black table he intended to use for the altar, he had forced some of his victims to pose for pictures.

The bedroom would reveal more of the killer's activities. On the wall at the head of the bed was a blood stain in the shape of a half circle. When the police removed the bedsheet, they found that the mattress was drenched in blood.

Among much more damning evidence, the police would also find ether and chloroform in the bathroom. These two substances were typically used as anesthesia, but Dahmer used a mixture of both to sedate and knock out some of his victims. Formaldehyde, a substance commonly used for preservation, was also found in the bathroom, in plain sight.

Many other objects found in the apartment helped sealed Dahmer's fate. Police found the blue drum filled with acid containing three human torsos, and the standalone freezer containing several body parts. In the refrigerator, more human remains were found wrapped carefully in plastic—like meat from a grocery store. Not far from these were the condiments Dahmer used to flavor the human meat, along with salt and pepper.

An interesting fact is that while Dahmer would be dubbed "The Milwaukee Cannibal," he would actually eat the remains of only two of his victims. Nevertheless, with the number of body parts he was storing, it was apparent that he distressingly intended to add to that number.

Chapter Nineteen:

Straight from the Monster's Mouth

The interviews Jeffrey Dahmer gave in the years following his arrest would provide the world with a horrifically sobering, surprisingly clear picture of the makings of a serial killer. He was known to speak candidly of his crimes, perhaps most famously in an interview with Stone Philips.

Sitting beside his father, who had a docile demeanor that very much resembled his own, Dahmer made no attempt to deny any of his crimes. Though his father visited him often in prison, this would be the first time they would be speaking about the more disturbing aspects of Jeffrey's life. Jeffrey talked about his childhood and when the morbid thoughts began, noting how he withdrew into his imagination instead of talking to his parents. He didn't know how to make sense of either his homosexuality or his growing obsession with death and violence, so he simply let the thoughts fester.

His father Lionel would also admit that even if his son had come out to him as a gay man, he would have strongly disapproved, as homosexuality went against his Christian beliefs.

Several doctors would also examine Dahmer in the course of his incarceration. They would explain the killer's desire to create a completely subservient "zombie" as his expression of a need to "satisfy his sexual need for a not-fully cooperative partner." Dahmer also stated that because he worked six days a week, it was too much trouble to find this ideal companion, and so he felt that he had to create one.

In the Stone Philips interview, Dahmer himself would discuss that his crimes were about lust and control. There was no confusion about this at all, and when asked about the murder aspect, he would say, "The killing was just a means to an end. I didn't enjoy doing that." There seemed to be some truth to this as he was also known to have said that strangulation was his preferred method because, as strange as it may sound, he felt that it was the most humane way to end his victims' lives.

He also admitted that cutting up the bodies gave him sexual satisfaction. It fed into his desire for absolute control and was another stage in the deviant behavior that satisfied his insatiable urges—urges that only escalated with every grim milestone.

And cannibalism was the next phase. Consuming his victims made him feel like they became a permanent part of him, physically and spiritually, making it impossible for them to abandon him, just as his parents had when he was a teenager.

During these interviews, Dahmer showed little to no difficulty confessing and talking about his crimes. A Milwaukee Deputy Chief would make the same observation, saying that Dahmer "talks about killing people as if it's just like pouring a glass of water."

This sobriety, the clear way he narrated his crimes, would also render his insanity defense difficult to believe. Dahmer had pleaded guilty but insane in all but two of his seventeen murders; he could not after all explain all the evidence in his apartment as well as the testimonies from witnesses. The jury would deliberate for over ten hours before finding him to be sane in all of the killings.

The fact that he was so forthcoming even about the grisly details of his crimes also distinguished Dahmer from other serial killers. While he was a practiced liar, as was necessary to avoid detection all those years, he seemed to have been relieved at his unmasking, answering questions directly and taking accountability for his actions. He refused to blame what he had become on his parents or his less-than-perfect upbringing.

Upon examination, it also seemed that he had a conscience, which was why he self-medicated with alcohol. He was wracked with guilt, indicating that he could very well differentiate right from wrong past a cerebral level. This was an aberration in the general profile of serial killers that had been formed up until that point—sociopaths were not supposed to have empathy.

Remorse, however, would be more difficult to determine. "I'm glad that it's over," Dahmer said in the Stone Philips interview. "Any word I say to the victims' families is just going to seem trite and empty. I don't know how to express the regret—the sorrow that I feel for what I've done—for their sons. I can't find the right words." Whether or not there was any sincerity behind the words and the dead eyes, the world could only guess

Chapter Twenty:

Surviving Dahmer

Seventeen is the official number of men that Dahmer killed in a span of thirteen years. In uncertain terms, there could be more than what authorities were able to discover and more than what Dahmer wanted to admit to. What was undeniably certain was that there were two victims who survived Dahmer's twisted modus operandi. Just like the victims who were disemboweled or eaten, they were not spared from the abuse; the only difference was that they lived to tell the tale.

Preston Davis had the unfortunate chance of meeting Dahmer when they were both in Germany during their stint in the military. He was 20 years old when they crossed paths. Being a black man, Davis was instantly repulsed by Dahmer's racist tirades. When sober, Dahmer was tolerable, but when drunk out of his mind, he became insufferable.

Dahmer had killed his first known victim just a year before he was shipped out to Germany. When inebriated, he had zero inhibitions and would brag about killing a guy in Ohio. The men in the barracks knew nothing about him so they didn't believe him and dismissed the claim as just the alcohol talking. Alcohol made Dahmer turn into his evil alter ego.

Davis and Dahmer's first real encounter was in October 1979 when they took part in a field exercise in Belgium. When their vehicle broke down within three days of completing their mission, Dahmer took that opportunity to drug and sexually assault Davis. It was an incident that Dahmer did not admit to doing, but Davis insisted that it happened and the only reason why Dahmer didn't kill him was that he didn't know how to get back to Germany on his own.

Because of the traumatic experience, Davis blocked out the incident until it all came back to haunt him in 2009, when he was already 50 years old. He sought help from a therapist who specialized in military sexual trauma. During his treatment, his memory of another incident came to him—that Dahmer beat the hell out of him in an altercation during their military training.

Billy Capshaw had a more harrowing experience with Dahmer upon joining the same unit in Germany from 1979 to 1981 at just 17 years old. Dahmer had more access to Capshaw because they were roommates.

When Dahmer was sober, he was portrayed as a likable and charismatic person, but when he was under the influence of alcohol, he transformed into a sociopath with no conscience. He started controlling Capshaw by regularly beating him up. It was not some run of the mill physical beating; it was a beating of the most brutal kind. Dahmer would hit Capshaw's joints, knuckles, and shins with an iron bar. The pain was so severe that Dahmer would bring Capshaw to the doctor. Dahmer used this opportunity to convince the doctor that he was taking care of Capshaw.

Only one doctor became suspicious of Dahmer and believed that he was the one causing the injury. The concerned doctor advised Capshaw to report the matter to the authorities. Unfortunately, the complaint had fallen on deaf ears. Instead of setting things right, his superiors called Capshaw a "pussy" for complaining.

Because the people in authority did not take Capshaw seriously, it allowed Dahmer to carry out more abuses. He started to control Capshaw like his own submissive slave. He made sure that Capshaw didn't get regular assignments so he could lock the young man in the room. He also prevented him from taking phone calls and receiving emails from family members. At one point, Capshaw was listed as AWOL even though he couldn't leave the base because he was locked in the room.

When Billy had the opportunity to escape, he did so by going out of the window. He was able to spend a few nights in a hotel while he was still receiving his salary, but when the money ran out, he had no other recourse but to return to base. He was ruthlessly beaten by Dahmer as punishment.

Realizing that he could die in the hands of his sadistic tormentor, Capshaw learned Dahmer's moods and tendencies so that the attacks could be minimized. Dahmer would hit him harder when he cried or screamed, so he tried not to do either, even when the pain was too much to bear.

Capshaw suspected that Dahmer drugged him on many occasions because he would wake up all tied up and unable to get loose. Whilst in such helpless positions, Dahmer would forcefully sodomize Capshaw. He also recalled being choked until he fell into unconsciousness.

With the constant abuse, Capshaw started to feel numb inside. He had planned on killing Dahmer but wanted it to look like an accident. There were many opportunities to do it because Dahmer would always drink himself into an unconscious state. However, Capshaw felt that he wouldn't be able to get away with murdering his tormentor. If convicted, he would be imprisoned in Europe and would never see his family again. Although he felt that it was the right decision, he regretted not killing Dahmer when he had the chance.

Despite the physical and sexual abuse, Dahmer had professed his love for Capshaw. This created confusion in Capshaw's mind and perhaps contributed to the *Stockholm Syndrome* that prevented him from actually confronting and killing Dahmer. It was possible that Capshaw had developed feelings towards Dahmer because the captor-captive relationship had an element of small kindness – that of the captor letting the captive live.

Capshaw was isolated from other people, which barred him from getting perspectives and ideas other than his captor's viewpoint. The more he was detached from normality, the more he believed his inability to escape from the clutches of Dahmer.

All attempts to retrieve assistance were ignored. Capshaw's request to be transferred to another room was shot down even though the black eyes and the severe injuries should have been enough reason to approve his request. His liberation came from a field assignment that kept him far away from Dahmer. When he finally returned to base, Capshaw was unbelievably relieved that his tormentor had departed.

Davis and Capshaw were kept alive not by some stroke of chance, but because Dahmer was pushed into a situation where he couldn't carry out his plan without getting caught. In a huge way, being in the military environment provided Davis and Capshaw the cloak of protection from certain death.

Ironically, in the same vein, the military had failed to protect Davis and Capshaw from the sexual assault and physical abuses. It took repeated requests and calls for help before the military even heeded Capshaw's complaints. Initially they did not believe him and to prove that he wasn't telling the truth, they sent him to the dispensary to undergo a rape kit exam. Even with the results proving that he had been telling the truth all along, the doctor simply sent him back to his room.

Had someone from the unit showed even a shred of compassion, Capshaw wouldn't have had to endure 17 more months of rape and torture in the hands of Dahmer. What was jarring was that Dahmer was kicked out of the military because of alcohol abuse and not for the horrific deeds he enacted on Capshaw.

This exposed the US military's dirty secret that had been going on for a long time—that sexual abuse was a normal occurrence—the people of authority sadly turned a blind eye on. By ignoring Capshaw's grievances, the military allowed the sexual torture to occur right under their noses.

The most shocking realization is that the predatory acts were committed by one of their own. By dismissing legitimate complaints about sexual abuse, the military created an environment that discouraged the men in their stead to report crimes committed against them by their superiors or colleagues

Chapter Twenty-One:

Complicit Racism in Milwaukee During Dahmer's Horrific Spree

The gruesome murders perpetrated by Dahmer were a horrible reminder of how racially segregated Milwaukee was during his killing spree from 1978 to 1991. Most of Dahmer's victims were black men whom he targeted because they fit within his criteria—easy to manipulate and less likely to attract police attention.

Historically, Milwaukee was slow to attract African-Americans from the South because of its predominantly European immigrants. By the time blacks arrived in droves in the 1960s, the city's economy was in shambles largely due to the collapse of the city's industrial base. The black community didn't have the opportunity to develop their own middle class, much less an elite class, because their arrival in the city was blamed for its economic woes.

To make things even more difficult for African-Americans, the Germans, Poles, and Jews strongly opposed housing and school integration, which created more tension and divisiveness. Because of social and economic pressure, the black ghetto substantially declined. This made it easier for the white Milwaukee residents to write off the black community.

To this day, Milwaukee is the most segregated city in the United States with the highest black-white segregation index score. Statistically, Milwaukee is one of the worst places to live in for African-Americans.

Dahmer's trial not only revealed details of horrific murders, but it also exposed the racism that persisted in the city. The fact that 11 of the 17 victims were black raised the question of whether Dahmer's murders were racially motivated. By his own admission, Dahmer insisted that he selected his targets based on physical attributes and not on racial backgrounds however.

It can be argued that Dahmer chose his victims based largely on the physical features that so happened to be prevalent in black men. And since he lived in a predominantly black neighborhood, it was easy pickings. However, Dahmer may not have been aware that his actions and murderous intent were already racialized by the media. Although he had said that his actions were not racially motivated, anecdotal evidence suggested otherwise. There was a possibility that he had lied about his selection process because he wanted to be politically correct about the issue.

Even Dahmer's acquaintances knew about his hatred for black people, most especially black gay men. He would become notorious for his racist slurs. This was evidently contrary to what he said about his actions not being racist, when the fact of the matter was that he was consciously luring and baiting black gay men. It was impossible to ignore the racial aspect of the killing because Dahmer deliberately chose his victims based on race.

Dahmer was unmistakably aware that having minorities as victims would likely give him a better chance to get away with his evil deeds because minorities didn't attract as much attention from the police. This was evident in the case of Dahmer's Laotian victim Konerak Sinthasomphone.

Dahmer used his "white privilege" to get himself out of a sticky situations. Milwaukee police officers Joseph Gabrish and John Balcerzak bought in to Dahmer's narrative and surrendered Sinthasomphone to him without doing a background check on Dahmer or the boy— even a perfunctory search would have revealed that Dahmer was a registered sex offender and that Sinthasomphone was underage. The police officers were then reported to have made racist and homophobic jokes about the incident to the dispatcher.

What the incident confirmed is that there was a level of complicit racism in Milwaukee during that time period and it was magnified tenfold during Dahmer's trial. Dahmer was not the only monster in the grisly narrative. Victims had to grapple with the systemic bigotry and racism that spread through the country's criminal justice system.

The gross negligence of the police officers was the result of personal and institutional racism that existed in the city. They were quick to judge because of racial profiling—that the people involved fit a certain profile. To them, there was no reason to suspect Dahmer because he was white and there was no reason to believe Sinthasomphone because he was Asian. The police simply dismissed the incident as a domestic quarrel involving gay lovers and nothing more.

Gabrish defended the decision to give the young boy back to Dahmer because the officers saw a caring relationship between Dahmer and the Laotian boy and did not see any pressing reason to intervene in what they perceived as a lovers' dispute. What was even more absurd was that they didn't see something out of the ordinary even though the apartment where Dahmer lived had a foul smell because of the decaying remains scattered throughout the apartment.

Dahmer's trial put the spotlight on racism in Milwaukee like never before. The families of the 11 black victims issued a formal complaint listing down blatant examples of racism observed in the trial. They criticized the court system for treating Dahmer with deference, while the victims and their families were treated with disrespect.

The director of social service agency, Jeannetta Robinson, joined the victims' families in complaining about the jury selection. Among the 13 jurors, only one member was black. Furthermore, Robinson and the other counselors were not given passes to the trial.

The families also criticized the Milwaukee County Circuit Judge Laurence Gram, Jr. for allowing a defense request to allow Dahmer to smoke in jail despite regulations prohibiting it.

Unfortunately for the complainants, each protest was addressed sensibly and convincingly. For the jury selection, Milwaukee civil rights lawyer Arthur Heitzer explained that African-Americans and other minorities tended to be underrepresented in juries because they are less likely to be registered voters. With regard to the smoking complaint, Judge Gram relented to the request because Dahmer's psychiatrists and lawyers said that they can only perform their function if Dahmer is offered some cigarettes. The complaints were effectively shot down.

To add insult to injury, the two police officers, Balcerzak and Gabrish, who were fired from the Milwaukee Police Department were reinstated after filing an appeal and took on high-profile positions later in their careers. Gabrish became the police chief in Trenton, Wisconsin, while Balcerzak became the president of the Milwaukee Police Association.

Dahmer's trial may have exposed the blatant racism and bigotry involved in handling the case, but it did nothing to change the status quo. If anything, it only substantiated the claims that racism is pervasive in the criminal justice system in Milwaukee.

Chapter Twenty-Two:

Homophobic Hostility

There was no way to know with absolute certainty what Dahmer thought or felt when he carried out his heinous crimes. But what was palpable at the height of the case was the outbreak of hostility towards homosexuals. The gay community in Milwaukee was put in the spotlight in the most negative way imaginable. Anti-gay organizations found an irrevocable "proof" that homosexuals are the bane of humanity that spread evil wherever they go.

The fact that Dahmer, a gay individual, would terrorize gay men alike to him reinforced the homophobic ideology—that homosexuals are homicidal and evil. Gay and lesbian murderers were considered the villains of humanity and thus must be denied civil rights.

Anti-gay proponents such as the Family Research Institute published Paul Cameron's anti-gay sentiments to give their homophobic assertions some credence. They concluded that the violence involving gays and lesbians is self-induced, which is the argument they used to convince Congress that hate crime legislation should not be passed.

Cameron's studies have always been anti-gay, claiming that homosexuals are a threat to public health and well-being of children. His controversial research and conclusions were not shared by the scientific community and were largely ignored because he was ill-equipped and lacked the training to conduct rigorous scrutiny of a complex concern. Despite this, the damage has already been done. The anti-gay movement had found what they considered to be all the evidence they needed to link sexual violence and deviancy to homosexuality.

Dahmer's case was a shining moment for the bigots and the racists, with Dahmer's crimes being extremely gory and horrific. The protesters changed the narrative to convince the public that gay people and lesbians practice violent sex to their 'own kind'. It worked to some extent because people started associating sex crimes with gay people, which directed anger and resentment towards the gay community. Dahmer's sex crimes, violence, and cannibalism propagated the false assumption that extreme violence is a regular part of homosexuality.

Families of Dahmer's victims have said time and time again that the Milwaukee Police Department was indifferent towards the disappearances of their sons/brothers. They say that when the police found out that a victim was gay, there was always a quick change in attitude –up to the point that they became dismissive and contemptuous—a conduct unbecoming of police officers.

The hostility towards homosexuals was also implicit in some ways. When it became apparent that there was a pattern of disappearances of homosexuals who were regular patrons of gay bars in Milwaukee's east side, the search for them became almost nonexistent. In the rare chance that a missing gay person was reported, it wouldn't even be recorded. There was just no effort to look for missing gay men.

Had the police showed even one iota of interest in searching for the missing gay men, it wouldn't have been so hard to figure out that their disappearances all had connections to Dahmer.

Attempts to explain Dahmer's murder spree led to the conclusion that it was his internalized homophobia that compelled him to commit gruesome murders again and again. Some people speculate that Dahmer loathed his own homosexuality and the only way to assuage his guilt for being gay is to murder his own kind. Because the guilt did not vanish with every kill, he continued to murder hoping to find the satisfaction that he sought. Had he not been caught, Dahmer would have continued to kill without a doubt.

What psychologists, true crime writers, and the public simply accepted was that Dahmer's internalized homophobia was a natural psychological response to homosexuality. They failed to dig deeper and find the social context and origins of his homophobia. In a way, they didn't want to implicate American society as one of the reasons why Dahmer loathed his homosexuality. It would have been less homophobic to look into the reasons why Dahmer hated other homosexuals, but it was not the narrative that the anti-gay movement wanted to hear. They'd much rather want to blame homosexual people for simply being homosexual. After all, it appealed to the public's thirst for controversy and scandal.

It cannot be conclusively asserted that Dahmer's homosexuality crafted him into a serial killer, but the overwhelming evidence of his internalized homophobia could have quite possibly turned him into a murderous man. This internalized homophobia could very well have societal origins as he felt ashamed and guilty for being gay. His hatred of homosexuality gave him the urge to kill gay men who satisfied his sexual desires. It was one big confliction. If his homosexuality was taken out of the narrative, Dahmer would have been constructed simply as a deranged monster who killed men. American society could not be directly implicated in his crimes, because there would have been no causality to begin with.

Ironically, even though Dahmer hated his homosexuality, he used it to his advantage in at least two occasions. First when he was convicted of sexual assault in 1989 for seducing a child to do immoral acts. He asked the judge for leniency and used the "gay card" to procure a lesser sentence. Two years, later, he again told the police he was gay and the 14-year old boy who was running around naked in handcuffs was his lover. Clearly, Dahmer had no trouble admitting he was gay if it meant he could get away with his crimes.

Further complications arose when crime reporter Anne Schwartz attempted to exonerate the Milwaukee police officers from their inappropriate handling of the case involving the 14-year-old Sinthasomphone. In a shocking move, Schwartz published the criminal records of every murdered victim of Dahmer in an effort to demonize them. By doing this, Schwartz represented homosexuality in a demeaning and disrespectful way. It made the largely homophobic readership less sympathetic to the gay victims and more sympathetic to the racist and bigoted police officers—and to Dahmer, to a certain extent.

Schwartz created a false perception of the Milwaukee police officers as being tolerant of homosexuals and blacks, when their actions showed otherwise. It was a clear manipulation of narratives to push for a racist and homophobic agenda.

Dahmer's case reinforced the notion that homophobia and racism in Milwaukee are mutually dependent especially as they pertain to victims of crimes. Dahmer expressed his internalized homophobia by killing mostly black gay men, but the media and the police refused to portray him as a homosexual. There was no explicit declaration of his homosexuality because the complex interplay of homophobia and racism would be brought into the mainstream and into the public consciousness. It would have presented complication for the simple reason that Dahmer, the real villain of the story, was white and gay. It was unfathomable at that time that the gay villain was white.

Even Dahmer's father, Lionel, did not mention his son's homosexuality until half-way through his book, *A Father's Story*. This is because he knew that his son would be further demonized because of his homosexuality—a testament to the rampaging homophobic hostility in Milwaukee at the time of the investigation and trial.

What can be gleaned from the interplay of homophobic discourses is that Dahmer grew up in an environment where homophobia may have influenced his thinking about sexuality and crimes. Towards the end of his trial, he started to create a link between the two. He acknowledged that he was sick because the doctors told him about his sickness. Although still elusive and somewhat cryptic in his statements, Dahmer could have been referring to his homosexuality more than his crimes.

The judge who handled Dahmer's insanity trial may have also subscribed to the belief that Dahmer's homosexuality, criminality, and insanity were intertwined, ordering him to undergo a brain scan. To the uninitiated, this may just be a normal examination to determine if Dahmer was criminally insane. However, historically, scientific examinations of this nature were conducted by homophobic scientists who wanted to pathologize homosexuality and deem it a medical abnormality.

It was evident that reporters, writers, and lawyers made efforts to "degay" Dahmer throughout the course of the trial, largely to avoid anti-homophobic sentiments. However, such efforts were thwarted by the fact that it was impossible to separate Dahmer's crimes with his hatred of his own homosexuality. An unfortunate consequence of this was that his victims' homosexuality was also hidden or erased, or at least downplayed. This is because if Dahmer was denounced for his homosexuality, it also presented his victims in a bad light.

Even the families of the victims were caught in their own homophobia by quoting a Biblical verse to denounce Dahmer's crimes and homosexuality, which effectively denounced the homosexuality of their family members. It was a way to normalize their queer sons, but whether it was intentional or a Freudian slip is a trivial matter to pursue.

Dahmer's victims may have hidden their homosexuality to their families that's why it created incongruence when families unwittingly denounced their sons' homosexuality. Whatever the case, it was evident that the larger problem was the institutional homophobia that persisted at that time and the subsequent gay-bashing that ensued.

Extreme groups had even stated that Dahmer did a great service to society by murdering homosexuals, oblivious to the fact that the man they were putting on a pedestal was a gay man himself. They weren't aware because Dahmer as previously mentioned was rarely presented as gay in news reports. The denial of his homosexuality is part of the fabric of institutional homophobia that is partly to blame for Dahmer's gruesome murders in the first place

Chapter Twenty-Three:

Defending the Indefensible

A t the heart of the insanity defense is the moral principle that individuals should not be punished for criminal acts committed when they have no control of their behavior because their ability to engage in rational thinking is impeded by a mental defect.

In Dahmer's case, if it is proven that he lacked the mental capacity to appreciate the wrongfulness of his actions or he lacked the capacity to act in conformity to the requirements of law, then he should be acquitted on the basis of insanity. This unenviable task landed on the lap of Gerald "Jerry" Boyle, Dahmer's attorney. To defend the indefensible is a job that no attorney would willingly take. But as fate would have it, Boyle was asked to take the case and he did not see any reason not to accept it.

It was not the first time Boyle handled Dahmer's case. In fact, they had a history together when Boyle represented Dahmer in 1988 after he was arrested for drugging, fondling, and photographing a 13-year-old boy. Dahmer pleaded guilty to the charges of second-degree sexual assault. During the sentencing, the prosecution represented by Assistant District Atty. Gale Shelton asked for a long prison term.

Boyle, as any defense attorney would do in that situation, asked for leniency on the strength of Dahmer's clean record at the time. Boyle told the judge that Dahmer wasn't a multiple offender and deserved a more lenient sentence.

At that time, Boyle had no idea that Dahmer had already killed five men, one of them just two months before he molested the child. No one suspected that Dahmer had already been on a killing spree. And yet he had the audacity to beg the Circuit Judge William D. Gardner not to destroy his life.

Judge Gardner saw the merit of Dahmer's plea and sentenced him to five years for sexual assault and three years for enticing a child for immoral purposes. The judge really believed that Dahmer would not receive the treatment he required if he was sent to prison. The judge renounced both sentences and instead ordered Dahmer to serve a one-year sentence in the county House of Corrections. It allowed him to hold his job at Ambrosia Chocolate Co. under a work-release program. He was also ordered to enroll in counseling and remain on probation for five years.

The leniency continued and Dahmer was released in March 1990 after only spending 10 months in the House of Corrections. It was two months early and it only took two months for Dahmer to go on another killing spree. Because of the leniency extended to him, he victimized and killed 12 more men before he was caught and arrested anew.

In hindsight, there was a public outcry after Dahmer was given what many people thought was a slap on the wrist. Boyle begged to differ. While it was most unfortunate that Dahmer killed after he was released, his stay in the House of Corrections was not a cake walk. Boyle argued that Dahmer served his time and behaved in accordance with the rules. Had Dahmer breached the terms of his probation, his probation officer would have sent him to prison for eight years. It wouldn't have made any difference if he was on probation or served the maximum sentence, because Dahmer would still kill either way.

Boyle is low-key and friendly, but he is one of the fiercest and most high-profile defense lawyers in Wisconsin. His career had always been in an upward trajectory ever since he graduated from Marquette

Law School in 1962. Early in his career, he prosecuted Milwaukee's first serial killer Michael Lee Herrington in 1967 and he never lost a single case as a criminal attorney.

Dahmer's father, Lionel, knew it was going to be tough finding a good lawyer to handle his son's case. The obvious choice was Boyle because he has been known to have handled the most controversial cases in Wisconsin. He had represented those who were accused of murder, drug dealing, and child abuse. He was also known for taking police brutality cases. Taking Dahmer's case was right up his alley so to speak.

Boyle is a consummate lawyer who mastered the art of cross-examination and closing argument. He could read witnesses with accuracy and at the same time, he could communicate with them effectively and coax them to spit out the truth. With his remarkable memory, he could piece together a story that jurors could grasp and relate to. Even the most complicated cases are broken down to easy-to-understand narratives. He had the knack for simplifying complex situations and a way with words.

Boyle's relationship with Dahmer was strictly on an attorney-client level. Boyle didn't want to become emotionally involved because he knew feelings could change the way he viewed his client. He had represented people accused of the most heinous crimes imaginable and many of whom were found guilty by the court. He also prosecuted many of them with favorable outcomes. He felt it was his job to take a step back and divorce himself from any emotion and focus on the facts of the case. Especially in Dahmer's case, it was important for Boyle to think of him as a client and ignore the public's perception of Dahmer as the monster he was.

Even before Boyle was retained as the defense attorney, Dahmer had already admitted to killing 17 men. His guilt was no longer in question because he already pleaded guilty by reason of insanity. It was up to Boyle to prove to the court and the jury that Dahmer committed the murders because he was insane. It was the appropriate legal defense for Dahmer especially when there was no sympathy for him because of the hideousness of his crimes.

Boyle was cognizant of the fact that it was a tough sell to the jury, but if he could convince them, it would make a tremendous difference in Dahmer's life. Because Dahmer was charged with 15 counts of first-degree intentional homicide, he could face a mandatory life sentence for each count, which essentially is the maximum a person could get in the state of Wisconsin, a state that has no death penalty.

If Boyle could pull it off, Dahmer would be sent to a mental hospital instead of a prison. In this situation, Dahmer would receive treatment for one year, after which he would undergo a psychiatric evaluation. If Dahmer could convince the trial judge that he was no longer insane and no longer a threat to the public, he would be released. It was the outcome that Boyle wanted for his client.

Chapter Twenty-Four:

The Insanity Defense

J effrey Dahmer's sanity trial not only revealed horrific details about how he disemboweled, killed, and consumed some of his victims, but it also gave an insight into his bizarre reasons for doing so. In a grueling 17-hour interview, Dahmer disclosed to mental health experts that he performed crude lobotomies on four of his last victims using a drill.

Prosecution psychiatrist Dr. Frederick Fosdal testified that Dahmer had grown tired and weary of killing men and wanted a live partner who would stay with him and obey his every wish. Before experimenting with DIY lobotomies, the only way his victims would be compliant to his whims was to drug and kill them. However, disposing of the body became too exhausting and impractical as he killed more men. On several occasions, he found himself tripping over and stepping on the carcasses of his victims in his bathtub as he showered.

Dr. Fosdal was a frequent prosecution witness who hardly ever supported an insanity plea, but after much prodding from defense attorney Gerald Boyle, he admitted that Dahmer suffered from a mental disease. Boyle contended that Dahmer murdered his victims because he could not control the urge to engage in necrophilia, which was the basis for Dahmer pleading guilty by reason of insanity.

Although Dr. Fosdal conceded that Dahmer had a mental disease, he made clear that Dahmer was in complete control of himself when he killed and mutilated his victims. In fact, Dahmer had a concrete plan, albeit gruesome and bizarre. Dahmer admitted that he tried to look for ways not to kill his victims. He wanted to keep them alive but completely interactive. However, he also wanted them to behave based on his own terms. He decided that a crude lobotomy could be the solution to his problem.

Dr. Fosdal's testimony revealed that Dahmer was not exclusively necrophiliac. Dahmer knew that he was not a pure necrophiliac and he insisted that he wanted to keep them alive as long as possible to make the period of sexual availability longer. He was cognizant of the difference and used the drilling technique to keep them alive, albeit in a zombie-like state.

Boyle insisted that the fact that Dahmer thought about lobotomies was already a sign that Dahmer was deranged. It was a strong argument that Boyle wanted to impress upon the jurors so that Dahmer's state of mind can be seen as far from being sane. Dr. Fosdal destroyed the argument by saying that in the oft chance that the lobotomies worked, it would prove that Dahmer had found a solution to his problem. Had his operations became successful, he would have created a sex zombie that could satisfy him. Had it worked, Dahmer would have stopped killing. It was bizarre and whacky, but it was rational.

The next set of witnesses comprised of three police officers and two of Dahmer's former bosses at the Ambrosia Chocolate Co. where Dahmer worked for more than five years as a mixer. They all testified that Dahmer was cooperative, polite, and courteous. They didn't see signs that Dahmer had mental disorders. It was the final nail to the defense's coffin.

But was it all that simple? Contrary to public perception, Dahmer's trial was anything but simple. The defense carried the burden of proof to convince the jurors that Dahmer was insane as he had claimed to be and not a cold-blooded killer as he was perceived by the general public. The inconsistencies in testimonies and presentation of facts by the defense failed to string together a cohesive narrative that could persuade the jury of Dahmer's insanity.

To better understand the outcome of the infamous sanity trial, it's important to know what actually went down during the trial and appreciate the compelling situations that surrounded it. It is worth noting that how the case was presented somehow had an impact on the outcome of the trial. The presentations were as compelling as the content of the evidence itself.

In *State v. Dahmer*, the defense had one goal: to set up a series of conjectures that would convince the jury that Dahmer was insane at the time he committed all 15 murders. Outside the four walls of the courtroom, the popular assertion was that Dahmer would have to be insane to kill his victims, have sex with the dead bodies, mutilate them, and keep body parts as mementos. No sane person could do such depraved acts. However, in the courtroom, narratives could be tweaked to get more sympathy from the judge and the jurors.

Defense Attorney Gerald Boyle knew what his client was up against. He had to portray Dahmer as someone who was too mentally disturbed to be held responsible for his grave actions. To do so, Boyle had to be selective of what events and evidence he had to present to the court. He had to maneuver the defense in such a way that the representation of the events was closer to the main objective—even if it meant having a stripped-down representation and filtered version of what occurred. This proved to be a gargantuan task because prior to the trial, Dahmer had released statements stating that he had meticulously planned the killings, which was an unlikely behavior for someone who claimed to be insane and out of control.

For those outside looking in, the trial should have been a demonstration of a swift and simple court case because the defendant had already entered a guilty plea. There was no need to determine who killed the men nor figure out the circumstances that led to their deaths. There was no need for an elaborate presentation because the biggest mystery had already been solved.

What the trial needed to accomplish was to determine two things: 1) if Dahmer suffered from a mental disease; and 2) if his mental disease made him incapable of conforming his deeds and actions to the requirements of the law. Sentencing was not even a major issue because Dahmer would be locked up either in a mental facility or a prison. Either way, he would be banished from society.

What made it particularly difficult for the defense to prove Dahmer's mental defect was his proclivity for documenting his actions by taking photos and keeping body parts as mementos. This forced the defense to get creative and strategic at the same time.

Seeing how Dahmer could threaten the defense's desired outcome, because of the inconsistency of his words and his actions, the defense decided that Dahmer would not take the stand. He was not sworn as a witness and never spoke at his own trial. All his statements were read by the people who reported them—psychiatrists, psychologists, police detectives, and experts in their respective fields.

By not allowing Dahmer to testify at his own trial, the defense made the jury focus their attention on the stripped-down representation of Dahmer's earlier sworn statements. By not permitting each juror to observe Dahmer from the witness stand, the defense was able to restrict the flow of damning information. In a way, the defense orchestrated the concealment of facts that would have shown that Dahmer was anything but insane.

The trial lasted for 13 days and the jury had reached a decision in less than 24 hours. On February 15, 1992, the jury found that Dahmer did not suffer from a mental disease when he committed the 15 murders he pleaded guilty to.

Perhaps unbeknownst to the public, because the jury answered "no" to the question of whether Dahmer had a mental disease, the second question about his ability to conform his conduct to the requirements of law was effectively struck down.

The verdict was met with varying reactions, depending on which side a person identified with. On one hand, there was an appreciation of the verdict because Dahmer was adjudged as sane and was held accountable for his appalling actions that he meticulously planned, plotted, and executed. On the other hand, many were left confused and puzzled, prompting them to raise an important question: If Dahmer could rape, kill, disembowel, and eat his victims and be found sane, who then is insane?

It was difficult to give a straight answer for such a complex question in light of Dahmer's insanity trial, but what was clear was the dissonance between perceptions in the legal community, the medical community, and the public at large. In fact, the terms *mental disease* or *mental defect* may have legal meanings that don't exactly match with medical terms used by mental health professionals. As such, the jurors were instructed to draw their own opinions and conclusions based on the evidence provided. They were not to be limited or bound by medical definitions and labels. However, the jury is bound by the legal definition of the terms.

What this really meant was that the jury can disregard the opinions or findings of medical health professionals or experts if they deviate from the legal definitions. With this kind of special instruction, the significance of the kind of information the jurors receive was crucial to the defense's strategy. Boyle knew this and took advantage of it. That's why he controlled the information that he wanted the jury to have. This is by no means illegal or frowned upon. In fact, trial courts encourage and demand that prosecution and defense attorneys pare down the facts to avoid repetition. It's being done so as not to waste time and expedite the process.

The defense created an alternate reality while proclaiming a strategy of open disclosure. The guilty plea was contingent on Dahmer's statements before sentencing despite the fact that the juror never heard or viewed Dahmer on the witness stand. The defense knew that Dahmer's live testimony would not be congruent to the reality that they want to project to the jury. This strategy of concealment was meant to control Dahmer and hide the inconsistencies between his actions and his admissions.

It might be difficult to fathom why the jury found Dahmer to be sane despite his reprehensible behavior. Logic would dictate that the evidence painted Dahmer as a deranged man who was not in control of his mental faculties, thus, enough to be adjudged as insane. However, the jury was instructed to base their decision on the strength of the evidence and use their own reasoning as long as it falls within the legal boundaries. The law presumes that a defendant is sane until proven otherwise.

In Dahmer's case, the state of Wisconsin adopted the American Law Institute's Model Penal Code (ALI) test, which has cognitive elements and volitional stress. Under this test, Dahmer would not be held responsible for the crime he committed if his criminal conduct as a result of a mental defect lacked the capacity to recognize the wrongfulness of his action.

Unless the defense could prove to the jury's satisfaction that Dahmer had a disease of the mind that made him struggle to differentiate the wrong from the right, then he would not be found insane.

The defense faced the challenge of proving that a psychiatric condition or a mental disease exists because it affects a person's capacity to exercise rational choice. It's difficult to determine if a mental disease exists because it doesn't always have an organic beginning. It can develop early but would only be diagnosed later in life. Also, the methods used to diagnose mental and psychiatric illnesses are not as exact as the diagnosis for physical illnesses. There is a lack of standard to ascribe with precision what makes up a normal or healthy rationality.

Punishment can only be handed to Dahmer if he can be blamed for his action, which means it had to be proven that his behavior was a product of his choice. The defense argued that Dahmer's mental disease prevented him from exercising his rational choice. It had to contend with the positivist bias that if something cannot be measured, it could not possibly exist.

The defense also had to circumvent the prevailing notion that criminals use mental diseases and insanity pleas to avoid punishment. Furthermore, psychiatrists are generally mistrusted when they take the stand because of their differing and contradicting findings. Their testimonies tend to favor the side they represented.

It was clear then as it is today that the odds were stacked against the defense, but it didn't mean it was a lopsided trial. The fact that the Wisconsin Supreme Court allowed the inclusion of all evidence that would show the true mental condition of Dahmer at the time his crimes were committed gave the defense a lot of elbow room to maneuver a strategy. It essentially made all of Dahmer's behavior and conduct admissible as evidence. There was no restriction on what could be presented as proof of insanity within the given time frame. All the defense had to do was mine all the resources they had, choose those that will help the case, and present them convincingly to the jury.

While it was established that Dahmer had a highly unusual set of triggers to enact his sexual fantasies, it did not automatically mean that he was less able to control them. From a psychiatric perspective, Sigmund Freud had doubted claims that those who engage in necrophilia suffer from a mental defect. Although Freud's theories were not used by the prosecution, the conjecture would have weakened the argument of the defense that necrophiliacs cannot override their resistance to depraved sexual acts.

What hurt the defense were the detailed interviews Dahmer had with detectives and experts that investigated his cases. On several occasions, Dahmer had even repeatedly requested to speak with officers even when his attorneys were not present to filter his train of thoughts. In one interview, he owned up to his crimes and lamented that he could have made different choices. He unequivocally stated that he made the wrong choices. He conceded that if he had more motivation, he would have resorted to worthwhile acts to fill his time instead of wasting his life away with alcohol.

Even though the defense had a lot of weapons in its arsenal, Dahmer's confessions prevented the presentation of a watertight argument because the self-reported narrative that was established would only serve to contradict it. As a result—and perhaps a mistake— the defense used the testimonies of clinicians to give the insanity plea a respectable and professional façade in which to conceal the fact that Dahmer knew the right from the wrong but chose the latter anyway. The defense relied on the possibility of the jurors buying into the narrative that Dahmer was not in control of his mind as evidenced by his extremely bizarre and violent behavior.

The defense encased Dahmer's statements in sworn testimonies of clinicians and experts so that they would be impervious to challenge. Had Dahmer testified, his statements would be scrutinized, disputed, and destroyed by the prosecution. This is because Dahmer's self-assessment and self-report had questionable truthfulness because of the glaring inconsistencies in his retelling of events. He would be exposed to the jury and it would hurt the defense even more.

In the end, the defense's strategy faltered because of logical gaps, inconsistencies and failure to connect the insane personality with that of a person who functioned rationally when he interacted with other people. Making Dahmer a silent defendant did not strengthen the defense but weakened it more because the jury saw through the covert suppression of facts. The jury did not buy in to the context to which the defense built its arguments and found the prosecution's arguments more compelling and more transparent

Chapter Twenty-Five:

Expert Testimonies

Ultimately, the jury's perception of the truth was the version that mattered in Dahmer's insanity trial. Even if the defense crafted a discourse that sublimated the focus on parts of the story that were advantageous to Dahmer's case, the jury saw through the gaping holes and inconsistencies. But what was apparent was that Dahmer's life was seen by the jury through the lens of expert witnesses, including detectives, psychiatrists, and clinical psychologists.

While the expert witnesses gave an air of respectability and professionalism, their testimonies don't necessarily become gospel truths the moment they were uttered. What the defense wanted to present to the jury was that by giving Dahmer a different voice, his statements would come out as consistent and truthful. It painted him as someone who unburdened himself and revealed the macabre truth to experts no matter how ugly it was. By doing so, the defense asserted that Dahmer's statements support the plea of guilty by reason of insanity. However, the pieces of evidence presented by both sides do not support such an assertion.

Dahmer's multiple conflicting statements were evident when he recounted the murder of Stephen Hicks. His first statement related that he had sex with Hicks but they got into a fight which led to Hicks' death. Dahmer said he struck him with a barbell and Hicks died in the process. However, Dahmer's subsequent statements changed over time. In one version of the story, Dahmer said that they didn't engage in sex and that Hicks was not gay. In his conversation with an examining psychiatrist, Dahmer said that he strangled Hicks with a barbell and masturbated in front of the body. No oral sex occurred. In another statement, he detailed how he cut open Hick's belly and masturbated to it before cutting his head off.

Had Dahmer testified, his inconsistencies would be exposed for the jury to cast doubt on his truthfulness as a witness. But since Dahmer did not take the stand, a cross-examination to determine the veracity of his statements never came into fruition. There wasn't even a chance for that premise to develop in the first place. It was possible that Dahmer embellished many of the things he claimed to have done to make him appear more mentally ill than he really was. But since there was no opportunity to test the validity of his statements in court, the jury was given the impression that Dahmer was telling the truth—all because his statements came from the mouths of experts.

The defense relied on the psychiatric testimonies of expert witnesses to convince the jury that Dahmer had a mental disease. Dr. Fred Berlin, the Director of the Sexual Disorders Clinic at John Hopkins University testified that Dahmer was not able to conform his conduct to the requirements of law because he was suffering from paraphilia, which is a condition characterized by sexual urges and desires that may involve extreme sexual activities that may lead to dangerous outcomes. Specifically, that Dahmer was a necrophiliac.

Dr. Berlin established that Dahmer was afflicted with a cancer of the mind wherein Dahmer's freewill was breached. With necrophilia, the person has no control over what comes into his mind. The focus was on satisfying his morbid sexual desires.

Prosecution attorney E. Michael McCann did not try to demolish Dr. Berlin's testimony, instead, he attacked his competence and integrity by pointing out the errors in how he evaluated Dahmer. It turned out that Dr. Berlin only spent four hours and forty-five minutes to evaluate Dahmer. Out of that small window of time, only forty-five minutes were spent talking about family and personal life, which practically gave him only fifteen minutes to talk about each of the 15 murders committed by Dahmer. It appeared that the evaluation was done expeditiously and possibly haphazardly. It may not be the case, but the prosecution made it appear that way to the jury.

As the cross-examination of Dr. Berlin heated up, McCann was able to make him admit that Dahmer was a pathological liar. This was the breakthrough that McCann needed because it benefitted the prosecution immensely. By establishing that Dahmer was a liar, much of Dr. Berlin's testimony was destroyed because his findings and conclusions were based solely on his conversations with Dahmer.

When given the opportunity to explain further, Dr. Berlin clarified that even if Dahmer was a liar and that he could be manipulative and deceptive, it did not mean that he wasn't mentally ill. Although it was a possibility, the damage had already been done.

Another defense witness Dr. Judith Becker testified that several events during Dahmer's childhood had devasting effects on him, not just physically but also emotionally. The trauma resulted in an irreversible change in Dahmer's psyche. He developed into a very disturbed man who had distorted perceptions about the world. It made him interact less with people and when he did reach out, it was more like a predator looking for his prey. Although Dr. Becker was a professor at the University of Arizona who specialized in the diagnosis and treatment of paraphiliacs, her testimony was said to have little scientific basis.

Dr. Carl Wahlstrom's described Dahmer as someone with a long history of mental illness. Because it was left untreated for so long, he had become severely delusional. Wahlstrom pointed out Dahmer's desire to create a zombie who would be his long-term partner. His delusion took an extreme turn when he planned to build a temple of human remains that would bestow him magical powers. Eating parts of the victims gave him the intimacy that he never had because of his lack of interaction. That was the extent of his deranged and delusional mind.

Dr. Wahlstrom believed that Dahmer clearly suffered from a severe form of mental illness.

To ensure that the jury would be presented with an objective assessment of Dahmer's state of mind, the judge appointed two psychiatrists, Dr. George Palermo and Dr. Samuel Friedman.

Dr. Palermo, a forensic psychiatrist, concluded that Dahmer internalized hostile feelings resulting from being teased by his peers during his younger years. He was of the opinion that Dahmer never developed the ability to forge meaningful relationships and his homosexual desires had been stifled. The teasing and the bullying, coupled with his sexual frustration, contributed to his transformation into a sexual sadist. His internalized hostility and sexual desires became a conduit to which his destructive behavior and frustration were expressed.

Dr. Palermo clarified that Dahmer killed gay men because he wanted to get rid of the source of his homosexual attraction. By murdering them, Dahmer symbolically killed what he loathed about himself. He also added that there was no substantial evidence to support the assertion that Dahmer was a necrophile. His behavior did not exhibit any symptoms of someone suffering from necrophilia. Dr. Palermo's testimony practically shot down Dr. Becker's findings.

On the other hand, Dr. Friedman testified that Dahmer was sane because he had strategically planned all the murders. It was impossible for an insane person to make elaborate plans to murder multiple victims. It would take careful thought to achieve a diabolical and sinister objective. However, his testimony took a different turn and negated himself in the process. After the repeated line of questioning, he admitted that even though Dahmer exercised his freewill, it did not invalidate the possibility of a diagnosis of a mental disease. When asked to clarify, Dr. Friedman said that Dahmer's personality disorder is tantamount to mental illness.

Prosecution witness Dr. Frederick Fosdal insisted that Dahmer was a cruel and calculating killer who preyed on vulnerable men who needed money or were looking for anonymous sexual encounters. He described him as cold and unaffected by the heinousness and severity of his crimes. When the defense attorney asked if Dr. Fosdal believed that Dahmer was a necrophile, he answered in the affirmative but clarified that necrophilia is not his main sexual preference. However, he could not identify or describe Dahmer's condition.

When the defense read the various categories of disorders listed in the DSM-III-R, Dr. Fosdal conceded that Dahmer had a mental disease, but was not insane. He added that his mental disease did not interfere with his ability to conform to the requirements of the law.

Dr. Park Elliott Dietz's testimony described Dahmer's crimes as meticulously planned and not impulsive acts. Dahmer made efforts to ensure that his victims were alone so that there would be no witnesses to identify him. Dr. Dietz underscored the significance of alcohol in Dahmer's killing process. Drinking alcohol was necessary for Dahmer to overcome his inhibitions. He was only able to do the horrible things he did while intoxicated. If he was insane and completely not in control of his mental faculties, he would not have the need to drink alcohol.

Dr. Dietz also offered an explanation on why Dahmer masturbated while holding the victim's severed head in one hand. He said that it symbolically facilitated the fantasy of having sex with the whole person, practically cutting out the awareness that the body was not attached to it.

Dietz's conclusion was particularly damaging to the defense because Dahmer's behavior was attributed to alcohol intoxication and not to a mental disease. It was not his mind that made him not conform to the requirements of the law. Although Dahmer had an abnormality of mind, it did not substantially affect his mental process.

The defense attempted to destroy the argument by asking Dr. Dietz if the murder would have stopped if Dahmer simply stopped drinking alcohol. Dr. Dietz was not able to provide a clear and adequate answer to the question, but he stood firm in his belief that Dahmer had a mental defect, exacerbated by alcohol abuse, but it did not qualify as insanity.

What the trial showed were a group of experts in the same field who haeld extremely varying opinions about Dahmer's mental state. It proved that there was no standard evaluation that would make them agree to a unanimous diagnosis. Though they conceded to Dahmer having a mental disease, they were not unified in their evaluation of his mental state. The objective of the trial was to determine whether Dahmer was insane at the time he committed his crimes. Establishing that he had a mental defect was not enough to conclude that he was insane.

This made the job of the jury even more difficult and they had to rely on how they interpreted the testimonies of the experts and connect it logically and sensibly to Dahmer's behavior. In the end, the jury rejected the argument that Dahmer was insane.

Although two of the 12 jurors found Dahmer insane, the Wisconsin state law requires 10 out of 12 jurors to return a verdict of insanity. Dahmer was sentenced to 15 consecutive life terms; one for each of the men he brutally slaughtered

Chapter Twenty-Six:

The Prosecution Strategy

While the defense presented a sequence of events that attempted to convince the jury that Dahmer's bizarre and brutal behavior was a result of a mental disease that made him insane, the prosecution contextualized Dahmer's alleged insanity by presenting him as a complete man, instead of painting him as a man who masterminded a series of unfortunate and horrific events. The result was a much more logical and truthful presentation of a man in conflict with his own sexuality.

In retrospect, the defense crafted a flawed strategy because it was not able to reconcile the version of events with what historically occurred. It did not account for other aspects of Dahmer's life, like his ability to hold a job or maintaining a normal existence outside of his criminal acts. How Dahmer managed to become undetected for so many years was never addressed.

There were so many gaps in the defense's narrative that it made things even more difficult to figure out. The jury did not buy into the "insane narrative" because it appeared to hide Dahmer's guilt, instead of making the jurors understand Dahmer's motivations and compulsions.

The prosecution, on the other hand, countered the perception of Dahmer as a madman who was not in control of his actions. It was important for the prosecution to establish that Dahmer knew what he was doing and made efforts to take precautions to ensure that he would not get caught.

Dahmer was fully aware of the consequences of his actions but did not want to stop. He was cognizant of the fact that he had the ability to choose right from wrong. The prosecution reframed the defense's depiction of Dahmer and made it stick— that Dahmer was a man who carefully planned his moves.

Normalizing Dahmer provided a context that seamlessly fit into the prosecution's narrative, which presented Dahmer as someone who was normal, ordinary, and sane. This was done by asking all the witnesses the same set of questions to establish that they had spent a reasonable amount of time with the defendant to get a fair and truthful assessment of his life, personality, and behavior. The witnesses were then asked if Dahmer exhibited a bizarre behavior at any point in their interaction with him (e.g., incoherent answers, delusional thoughts, hallucinations, or incongruent responses). The answers were similar even though the witnesses interacted with Dahmer at different time periods.

Dahmer's apartment manager described him as a nice guy who had the neatest apartment unit he had ever seen. The manager had not observed any indication of peculiar behavior. In fact, he trusted Dahmer well enough to even ask him to become his business partner.

Dahmer's former boss at the Ambrosia Chocolate Co. described Dahmer as quiet and polite. In fact, Dahmer was able to mix 500 distinct chocolate recipes during his tenure, which is an indication that he had the ability to concentrate and execute complex tasks without any difficulty. There was no doubt that Dahmer was able to perform his job as a chocolate maker satisfactorily. He had a day job just like regular people.

A mix of police officers and acquaintances served as the second set of witnesses who had interacted with Dahmer or observed him near the times of his killing spree. The prosecution wanted to establish that even citizen witnesses did not see Dahmer display a behavior that could be construed as out of touch with reality.

When it was time to question the expert witnesses, the jury had already been introduced to a version of Dahmer who was normal and largely unremarkable that no one would suspect of any wrongdoing. Predictably, the expert witnesses corroborated the testimonies of the lay witnesses, which further strengthened the prosecution's case.

The knockout punch that the prosecution delivered was Dr. Dietz's expert opinion which served to establish that Dahmer's acts were all planned and deliberate. Dahmer would pulverize sleeping pills so that they would be easier to mix into a drink that he would serve to his victim.

Dahmer chose his victims well to make sure that the act would be discrete and wouldn't attract attention. He stayed away from men who had cars because he wanted to lure them to his apartment without the neighbors seeing. He only killed in his own apartment because it allowed him the control to execute his demonic plans. What's more, he only killed on weekends because it meant he could spend more time with the dead bodies. He could do anything he wanted without rushing his rituals because he didn't have to go to work.

The most telling testimony presented by the prosecution was that fact that Dahmer used a condom when he had sex with his victims— either with the corpse or with the helpless unconscious person. His reason was that he didn't want to contract sexually transmitted diseases such as HIV/AIDS. This destroyed Dahmer's assertion that he could not control his sexual desires as well as his aggression and violence. Dr. Dietz concluded that Dahmer had unorthodox sexual desires and longings, but his behavior did not meet the recognized criteria befitting someone who was insane.

The jury was compelled to believe the prosecution's assertions, contentions, and arguments because they were presented coherently and cohesively. The narrative that Dahmer functioned rationally in his interactions with other people was corroborated by the testimonies and the evidence presented. The prosecution succeeded in weaving a story that reconciled Dahmer's self-report and previous statements with what the witnesses observed about him. It was enough reason to convince the members of the jury that Jeffrey Dahmer was not insane and therefore must be held responsible and liable for his actions

Chapter Twenty-Seven:

Lionel Dahmer: A Father's Story

Trying to account for how things have turned awfully wrong in Dahmer's life was difficult for Lionel Dahmer. He had to look far back to trace how the malicious force inside his son had swallowed him whole.

When Jeffrey started his descent into madness, Lionel felt that the memories he had of his childhood were erased. The little things in his childhood that he thought were just normal activities seemed to have foreshadowed the evil Jeffrey created over the years. In retrospect, Lionel remembered that time he went to Iowa State University housing to clear out trash and debris. There was a putrid foul smell that permeated the basement, where he found the carcasses of small rodent like animals. He placed the bones and remains within a metal pail to have it disposed of.

What was an ordinary clean up turned out to be a forewarning of the evil that was to come decades later. Jeffrey was only four years old that time but he was fascinated and amused by the clanking sound of the bones hitting the metal pail. Lionel thought nothing of it because it was just like his son playing pickup sticks, but with bones.

At that time, Lionel didn't think that Jeffrey was overly fascinated or taken with it, but in retrospect, and in light of what had happened, Lionel started to think that it was a red flag that was unnoticed and simply ignored because it didn't mean a thing back then.

There were reels of homemade videos of Jeffrey that Lionel had transcribed. In a strange conversation, Jeffrey asked what would happen if his navel were cut out. Lionel just passed it off as one of those things the little kids ask out of curiosity and without malice. The same line of questioning happened when Jeffrey had a double hernia operation. He was overly concerned that his penis would be amputated.

Dahmer's stepmother Shari Dahmer met Jeffrey when he was 18 and he had just graduated from high school. At that time, Lionel was on the final stages of his divorce from Jeffrey's biological mother, Joyce. Shari and Jeffrey got along fine because he was able to separate his personal relationship with his biological mother from that of his stepmother. This was something that surprisingly came easy considering that Jeffrey was mostly withdrawn.

When asked if he was compelled to change the surname Dahmer just to get away from all the negative publicity and attention, Lionel said he's proud of the name and the ancestry. But he admitted that in certain cases, he and Shari would use a different name to avoid drawing too much attention, especially when eating in a restaurant. He felt that there was always some hesitation to use the name not because he was embarrassed by it, but because people had a morbid curiosity.

Shari married into the family but she was never embarrassed by the name that she acquired through her marriage to Lionel. She had always been proud to use the name in business and elsewhere. There was no compulsion to change the name as they didn't do anything wrong and there was no reason to be embarrassed about the name.

Jeffrey's brother, David, changed his name to remain anonymous and to distance himself from the controversy. To this day, David's new identity is completely secret and his family made sure it stays that way.

The only thing that Lionel and Shari were comfortable of disclosing is that David has a career and everything in his life is going well despite the terrible circumstances that befell the Dahmer family. For the most part, David succeeded in putting aside that unfortunate connection with his brother. It was his way of getting on with life away from the negative attention.

David and Jeffrey got along well, but the seven-year age difference was too significant a gap for them to develop the same interests. They grew up with different hobbies and pursuits and went out with different sets of friends. Their relationship cannot be described as close brothers, but they got along well enough to have a bond.

Lionel wrote a book and agreed to be interviewed on television by the likes of Oprah Winfrey and Larry King because he wanted to warn parents about the red flags of raising their children. Somehow, he might have regretted not seeing the signs when Jeffrey was just a little boy. He stated repeatedly that he had no other motivation for coming out on talk shows and writing his book other than to help parents. His intent was to prevent young kids from turning into serial killers or murderers in adulthood. Lionel believes that if troubled children get the help that they need early in life, their mental issues could be addressed properly.

Lionel was too caught up with his work that he failed to see the subtle signs exhibited by his troubled son. It didn't help that his marriage was falling apart when Jeffrey was just a young impressionable boy. Perhaps he believed that he had a sense of responsibility to parents as a way to compensate for his son's behavior. Of course, there's no way of knowing with certainty what his real motivations were, but he made it his advocacy to help parents do what he failed to do with his own son.

Unbeknownst to Lionel and to his ex-wife Joyce (now deceased), Jeffrey had been collecting dead animals between the age of 12 and 14. They both learned about the disturbing information only during the trial. While there is no evidence of blatant neglect on the part of Jeffrey's parents, it is safe to assume that Jeffrey must have spent much of his time alone and without adult supervision. Apparently, not even his friends knew about his unhealthy interest in road kills.

When Lionel learned of his son's strange behaviors through the testimonies and cross-examinations of expert witnesses, he had to think back to trace the beginnings of Jeffrey's derangement. Strangely though, Lionel had started keeping a journal to chronicle Jeffrey's development after he was born. It was as if he knew that he would have a need for it in the future to get an insight into his son's psychopathology.

The journal entries revealed Lionel's observations about his son. He described him as having emotionless facial expressions with motionless eye contact and mouth position. He also avoided direct eye contact with people he interacted with. Physically, his knees were locked and he would drag his feet when he walked, akin to a zombie lumbering around. He was also described as robotic. He didn't show emotions and he appeared to be unfeeling. Because of his inwardness, he was unable to establish relationships that were appropriate for his young age. As a result, he became reclusive and socially awkward.

As Jeffrey grew up, Lionel noticed that he was becoming more emotionally detached and he seemed to have developed a very limited range of emotion. He also did not show interest in activities introduced to him—things that kids would normally be interested in. But if there was one thing that he was interested in, it was dissecting animals. By the time he reached high school, he had already learned how to process dead animals.

Being a chemist, Lionel was actually pleased with his son's growing interest in chemicals. Little did Lionel know at that time that his son would soon learn to expertly use corrosive acids on human bodies that he collected.

Although Lionel had repeatedly said that he and his ex-wife didn't see signs of a troubled behavior in Jeffrey, the observations he wrote in his journal were a treasure trove of information hailing many red flags. There were plenty of signs from childhood to adolescence and well into adulthood, but no one—not even Lionel—expected anything.

It would be unfair to cast blame on Lionel or Joyce because they seem to be genuinely oblivious to what their son was up to until it was too late to help him. But it would appear that Lionel felt that he had a responsibility to share what he learned from the tragic events in the hope that parents would not ignore the signs that he did.

Chapter Twenty-Eight:

Deconstructing Dahmer

E ven after his conviction and death, Jeffrey Dahmer continues to fascinate and baffle researchers, criminologists, psychologists, and just about anyone interested in serial killers. Dahmer's case has been studied extensively from the time of his trial up to his incarceration and even decades after his death. With renewed interest in serial killers, Dahmer's name is brought back to the public's consciousness in an attempt to introduce the infamous Milwaukee Cannibal to a new generation of researchers.

Studies have attempted to analyze Dahmer to make sense of his obscene behavior. As expected, the scientific research community delivered. Numerous findings and conclusions surfaced, but there was really no consensus on what really turned an extremely shy boy into a monster.

Dahmer's case is unlike any other serial killers, not just because of the brutality and the cannibalism, but also because it encompassed the social constructs of gender and race. It was a complex interlink of issues that made it difficult to determine where Dahmer's behavior fit in the personality disorder spectrum.

A serial killer can originate from any background, age bracket, race, gender, and socio-economic status, but a common profile of a serial killer is that of a white male in his 20s or 30s with a history of childhood abuse and neglect, comes from a low-middle income family, is sociopathic or psychopathic, and appears normal to people he interacts with. By this definition, Dahmer fits the bill to a T.

Even though Dahmer exhibited the general traits that characterize a serial killer, it still does not explain why he turned out the way he did. There were numerous studies that attempted to deconstruct Dahmer just to determine the underlying issues that drove him to develop a compulsion to kill. One of the commonly used arguments is Dahmer's hatred of his own homosexuality. His aggression and violence towards his gay victims were said to be a release from his self-loathing. Believing in this is tantamount to reducing Dahmer into a racist and homophobic construct.

Research studies on serial killers largely focused on the biological and environmental development of the individual, and less on childhood component of the serial killer's growth. It's possible that Dahmer's psychopathy may have had its beginnings in childhood. A history of childhood neglect and childhood abuse could have had a long-term impact on Dahmer's emotional and social development. His unpleasant tendencies, that had formed into a horrific violent murder spree, could potentially be traced back to the events of his childhood at the tender age of six.

Childhood abuse pertains to any act by a parent, guardian, or caregiver that can result in physical, emotional, or psychological harm to a child. Children who experience abuse early in life may develop psychological and emotional trauma which could affect their development as adults. When not addressed or processed properly, children can develop an extreme response to the childhood abuse in the form of deviant behaviors and depravity.

Some types of abuse include physical abuse, sexual abuse, childhood neglect, and emotional abuse. Each of these types has differentiating effects on the child. Furthermore, the child has different ways of coping with the abuses. While some could handle the cards they are dealt with, many victims of childhood abuse end up with depression, anti-social disorders, suicidal thoughts, and other psychological disorders.

Research funded by the Canadian Department of Justice revealed that aside from the psychological consequences, there are gender-based risks that may arise from the abuses. Female victims of childhood abuse are more likely to internalize the experience, making them susceptible to developing eating disorders, suicidal ideation, and low self-esteem. On the other hand, male victims have the tendency to externalize the abuse by exhibiting aggressive and violent behaviors towards others.

Among the types of abuse, sexual abuse, childhood neglect, and emotional abuse can be applied in Dahmer's case to a large extent. Dahmer's childhood, as described by his family, was as normal as any other person's childhood. Based on outward appearance, Dahmer was a happy young boy raised by a loving family. However, interviews with his parents also revealed that there were family issues that may have contributed to Dahmer's personality and behavioral change.

Traumatizing events like his double hernia surgery terrified the then four-year-old boy because he thought that his penis would be amputated. Freudian psychology would view the castration as a foreshadowing of Dahmer cutting the penises off of some of his victims.

Dahmer's childhood may have been normal and unremarkable in the early years, but it turned dark and tumultuous fast when his parents' marital problems started to surface. His mother, Joyce, was heavily medicated with prescription drugs and struggled through her mental illness.

It was also revealed that while Joyce was pregnant with Jeffrey, she took 27 pills a day. It was a deadly mix of anti-anxiety drugs, relaxants, barbiturates, anti-depressants, growth hormones, and progesterone. She became addicted to tranquilizers because it somehow eased the debilitating effects of her psychological problems.

Calling her pregnancy difficult was an understatement. Aside from the pregnancy woes, Joyce had bouts of anxiety and dysphoria, which only worsened the marital discord later in her relationship. It was possible that the potent drugs in her system affected the development of the fetus. Joyce was also a germaphobe so she rarely had any physical contact with her son. The only time she had physical interaction with him was when she had to change his diaper.

Throughout his childhood, Dahmer frequently witnessed the verbal and physical altercations between his mother and father. Dahmer was trapped in a chaotic environment created by the breakdown of the marriage.

As years flew by, Lionel and Joyce became so caught up with their own lives that they ended up neglecting their son. With little interaction with his parents, Dahmer was mostly left to fend for himself at a young age. He was separated from his mother and younger brother when he moved with his father to Ohio. It was here, he felt even more alone and isolated because his father was so caught up with work. There is reason to believe that Dahmer developed abandonment issues when his parents divorced.

Lionel had told probation agents that his son was sexually abused by a young peer from the neighborhood when he was only eight years old. However, this was left unreported to the police and was only revealed two decades after it apparently occurred. Lionel and the police never divulged the real nature of the alleged abuse, but it happened while the Dahmers were still residing in Bath Township, Ohio. Lionel believed that it may be the reason why Dahmer had sexuality issues. Dahmer denied that he was molested by a neighbor, but if it were true, it may explain why Dahmer targeted boys and young men to torture, rape, and murder.

Since Dahmer never experienced violent physical abuse and the sexual abuse allegation was unsubstantiated, it is implied that the influencing factors for Dahmer's behavior were parental neglect and emotional abuse. Numerous studies have shown that early childhood abuse, in any form, is detrimental to a child's development. It can lead to anti-social behavior, aggression, and violent outbursts.

As Dahmer grew up, he withdrew from others and internalized his frustration. He did not seek help when he was old enough to do so. His father didn't see the signs or perhaps failed to acknowledge that there were issues that needed to be resolved. No one intervened or provided help because they only saw the shy and nice young man who didn't exhibit any form of deviant behavior—at least not in plain sight.

Childhood abuse and neglect are precursors to violent or anti-social behavior. True enough, Dahmer exhibited anti-social behavior. This behavior is a mental health condition that makes a person manipulate, exploit, and violate the rights of others. The earlier a child is exposed to abuse and neglect, the more likely he or she will engage in more serious behavior patterns in adulthood.

Based on Dahmer's behavioral patterns and tendencies, he was negatively affected by the divorce of his parents, the separation of the family, and the blatant neglect of his father. It led him to develop anti-social traits that made him devalue the lives of other people. As he got older, these traits developed into full-blown psychopathic tendencies, which eventually led to 17 gruesome murders that continue to haunt the victims' families.

It would appear that even before Dahmer was born, the odds were already stacked against him. Based on his father's journal entries after he was born, Jeffrey already showed signs of a troubled mind. According to psychiatrists, the observations (physical and emotional) were consistent with symptoms of Asperger's Disorder, which is a part of the autism spectrum. In fact, he was diagnosed with the disorder in one of his psychiatric evaluations.

Autism is one of several psychological disorders that have genetic roots. Neuroimaging studies have shown that people with autism are reported to have extensive developmental alterations within different parts of the brain including the amygdala, cerebellum, corpus callosum, and hippocampus.

So, it was also possible that his developmental and psychological behaviors may have developed while he was still in the womb, likely due to his mother's 27-pill regimen. This implies that Dahmer's homicidal and sadistic behaviors had biological roots. This is not to say that autism causes individuals to become homicidal; it just offers another theory that Dahmer may have developed neuropsychiatric abnormalities in utero.

Psychologists also put forward the theory of mental illness, which proposed that Dahmer's violent behavior is directly correlated to his mental illness. Although the jury did not find him insane, it did not change the fact that he suffered from several mental health disorders which were untreated because they were not previously diagnosed in the first place.

Before the start of the trial, Dahmer was diagnosed with borderline personality disorder, psychotic disorder, and schizotypal personality disorder. If the diagnoses were accurate, it is safe to say that Dahmer's deviant behaviors stemmed from personality disorders that had come from childhood trauma.

Dahmer's unstable moods, volatile behavior, stunted emotional growth, and inability to forge relationships were all the resultant effects of stressors inflicted upon him during his developmental years.

The emotional pain he endured when he was constantly teased by his peers was internalized until it begged for a release. The release is a way to transfer the pain he felt inside to someone else either by threatening physical harm or inflicting physical harm on others.

It is difficult to attribute a single cause for Dahmer's criminal behavior because there are always numerous factors and variables at play. But what can be safely concluded is that the complex combination of biological predisposition, childhood stressors, and parental neglect may have been the root cause of Dahmer's psychological disorders. Dahmer's coping mechanism became so extreme that he acted out his perverted fantasies and depraved sexual desires that left his victims dead and disemboweled

Chapter Twenty-Nine:

Dahmer Sympathizers

As strange as it may sound, many people feel sorry for Jeffrey Dahmer. How is it even possible to have sympathy for someone who viciously slaughtered seventeen men? Where is the compassion stemming from and why are people romanticizing a serial killer? To answer these burning questions, one has to believe that humans are intrinsically good until they do something bad—or in Dahmer's case, very, very evil.

Dahmer was not always wicked. He may have exhibited bizarre behavior early in life, but there were flashes of goodness and innocence in him. It was just unfortunate that his young life was quickly enveloped in to darkness when he succumbed to the allure of alcohol. It was tragic at how his alcohol abuse expedited his transformation from a shy young man into a monster.

Despite the severity of the crimes committed, people were much more understanding and sympathetic to what Dahmer had become. Dr. Samuel Friedman, one of the psychologists who testified in the trial, found Dahmer polite, courteous, charming, and pleasant to be with. He boldly stated that Dahmer, with his macabre methods, was not such a bad person.

There is this notion among Dahmer sympathizers that he was a victim of the environment he grew up in. It was easy to romanticize him because they proffered the narrative that Dahmer killed men as a desperate attempt to find love, closeness, and intimacy. Those who bought into this idea saw Dahmer as a helpless man who had a profound mental illness but no one stepped in to help.

They may have a distorted perception of Dahmer because they don't see him as the main source of evil. Instead, they see evil as something that was forced upon him and he had no way of escaping from it. To them, Dahmer was helpless from the elements that controlled him. Since he came from a dysfunctional family who neglected him, he had to escape somewhere to find the joy and satisfaction that he craved. It so happened that he found them by inflicting pain on others. Everything he internalized had found a release in extremely violent ways.

Perhaps the curious fascination with serial killers created the phenomenon of sympathizing with someone whose actions were extremely brutal and sickening. Dahmer reached celebrity status for all the wrong reasons, and yet there are Dahmer sympathizers and apologists who truly believe that the despicable things he did were only a means to an end.

Of course, Dahmer sympathizers do not proclaim that murdering victims is the right thing to do. They were just able to separate the man from his horrible crimes because they had developed an affinity to him by empathizing with him. Despite what had transpired, Dahmer was still a human being imprisoned by his mental defects.

A less profound way of looking at it is that many people tend to be drawn to personalities that are romanticized, especially in film and literature. Serial killers and mobsters are examples of these romantic figures. They are treated more like celebrities than the criminals that they truly are. The media—social media included—sensationalize their crimes and elevate their status, so it's easy to be blinded by the trappings of their celebrity and forget the gravity of their crimes.

The more people are taken in by Dahmer's narrative, the more they make excuses for his criminal behavior. For whatever reason, they shift to blame to something or someone else because in their minds, Dahmer was a victim first, and a serial killer, second

Epilogue

Jeffrey Dahmer was sentenced to 15 consecutive life sentences with no parole. He was given an additional life sentence for the killing of his first victim, Stephen Hicks.

Two years into his sentence, he requested to be baptized. Wisconsin minister Roy Ratcliff performed the baptism in 1994. Ratcliff truly believed that Dahmer was sincere in his desire to change. In their conversation, Dahmer bared his soul and confessed that he felt horrible for the things he had done. He added that he should have been put to death.

Dahmer asked if he is sinning against God by continuing to live. The pastor said that by continuing to live, he is submitting to the state, which means that he must obey the rules and not to undermine the system. Dahmer understood that he must accept his position as a prisoner of the state and serve God for as long as he lived, even if it meant staying in prison for the rest of his life.

Dahmer was on cleaning detail in a gymnasium bathroom at the Columbia Correctional Institute, a prison in Portage, Wisconsin. Left alone for a mere twenty minutes by the prison guards, Christopher Scarver, a twenty-five-year-old murderer who was both bipolar and schizophrenic, beat Dahmer to death with a steel bar. The weapon had been pilfered from the prison's weight room. By the time the guards found Dahmer, he had already been knocked unconscious, his head and face covered in a bloody mess. He would not make it to the hospital, dying of skull fractures and brain injuries on the way there.

Afterwards, thirty-seven-year-old Jesse Anderson, would also be attacked by Scarver, expiring two days later.

The motives for the murders were unclear, though it was suspected that one might have been a desire for infamy and attention. As Scarver was black and had landed in prison for murdering his coworker in a fit of anger over his boss' alleged racism, revenge for Dahmer's numerous black victims was also considered as a motive. Whatever the case, the jury was unconvinced of Scarver's insanity and ruled that he was guilty.

As he had died of head injuries, Dahmer's death bore some resemblance to his victims', whose names are unfortunately not as well known. They are often listed in the order of their deaths, their lives overshadowed by the circumstances of their passing. It is a sad and unfortunate legacy to simply be remembered as a victim of one of the worst serial killers the world had ever seen, despite one's accomplishments and contributions to society.

The victims' families would be severely impacted by the actions of one man, and many of them have chosen to keep the rest of their lives private instead of indulging the public's morbid curiosity regarding their lost loved ones.

Jeffrey Dahmer's legacy is a grisly chain of tragedy. The true rationale behind the psychology of serial killers remains a mystery, making stories like Dahmer's fascinating—but only for those fortunate enough never to have crossed his path.

Key Personalities: What Became of Them?

Lionel Dahmer is retired and still lives in Ohio. A portion of the proceeds of his book, _A Father's Story_, was donated to the families of the victims. Lionel and his second wife, Shari Dahmer, refused to change their last name. Despite what happened, they never stopped loving Jeffrey.

Joyce Flint (Jeffrey's mother) moved to California after the divorce. She visited Jeffrey several times in Wisconsin. She actively worked in the field of HIV and AIDS treatment. She died of breast cancer in year 2000 at the age of 64.

David Dahmer (Jeffrey's younger brother) chose to change his name and to live in anonymity with his own family.

Gerald Boyle (Dahmer's defense attorney) continued to practice law until his license was suspended by the state Supreme Court for medical incapacity, following an ethics complaint against him. He still strongly feels that Dahmer should have been sent to a psychiatric hospital instead of prison so that he could be studied in the hope that they'd find something that could help individuals with mental health problems.

Philip Arreola (former Milwaukee Police Chief) fired the two officers who mishandled the incident involving Dahmer and the ill-fated Konerak Sinthasomphone. The swift action, though lauded by the general public, caused tension in the department. He resigned from his post in 1996 to become the chief of Tacoma Police Department. He now serves as the Regional Director for the US Department of Justice CRS.

Officer John Balcerzak and Joseph Gabrish were fired from the Milwaukee Police Department but were reinstated following an appeal. Balcerzak became the police chief in Trenton, Wisconsin, and Gabrish continued to serve in the police force and was voted as police union president.

Preston Davis and Billy Capshaw are the two surviving victims of Dahmer while serving in the military. Both of them came out years after the abuse to talk about their harrowing experiences. Davis blocked the incident out of his mind for three decades, but it resurfaced once he saw Dahmer's name online. He had to undergo therapy. Capshaw, on the other hand, documented his ordeal and recovery on a website. He suffers from symptoms of PTSD and he said that it contributed to the failure of his marriage.

Christopher Scarver was convicted for killing Dahmer and another inmate. He was sentenced to two life sentences as a result of the two killings. While serving his time in the Columbia Correctional Institution, he was diagnosed with schizophrenia after complaining of having messianic delusions.

In 2015, Scarver came clean and revealed the reason why he murdered Dahmer. He explained that he had grown tired of Dahmer's antics, one of which including using prison food to create figures that would resemble limbs and drizzling ketchup over them to represent blood. Prisoners and the prison staff were repulsed by the behavior and they perceived it as Dahmer being unremorseful and unrepentant of his crimes.

Jeffrey Dahmer was announced dead on November 28, 1994